Tales from Hog Heaven

A Collection of the Greatest
Arkansas Football Stories Ever Told

By

Na

T0204336

Sports Publishing L.L.C.
www.sportspublishingllc.com

Director of production: Susan M. Moyer
Project manager: Jim Henehan
Dust jacket design: Deana Merrill
Developmental editor: Erin Linden-Levy
Copy editor: Cindy McNew

Cover photo courtesy of Tim Sharp, AP/Wide World Photos
Interior photos courtesy of Arkansas Media Relations

ISBN: 1-58261-345-1

Printed in the United States of America

Sports Publishing L.L.C.
www.sportspublishingllc.com

Dedication

To my beloved wife Nancy:

Without your encouragement and inspiration, this book never would have been attempted, much less written. I will love you until the 12th of Never and Beyond.

Acknowledgments

My thanks to *Hawgs Illustrated* editor Clay Henry, whose assigning me the "Where Are They Now" articles in *Hawgs Illustrated* provided much of the background and contacts concerning Razorbacks past. Also, I gratefully acknowledge the cooperation of Arkansas sports information director Kevin Trainor and former Arkansas sports information director Rick Schaeffer and their staffs. A huge thank-you to Jeff Jeffus, Jim Blankenship and Sandy Thompson of the *Northwest Arkansas Times* for the use of their facilities and to Sports Publishing editor Erin Linden-Levy for her patience.

To those who most influenced my career from my first boss, retired sports editor Wendell Redden of the *Joplin Globe*, former *Springdale News* sports editor Larry White who brought me to Arkansas, and the late Orville Henry and the late Bob Douglas, legends who will live forever in Arkansas journalism, thank you all.

Without you, there would be some 20 exasperated employment agents with wringing hands concurring, "There's nothing we can do with this guy."

And finally, thanks to Arkansas, the state that's held me like a magnet, a unique place of such diverse people uniquely united on a Hog Call.

Table of Contents

Fred Akers

A LONGHORN WHILE HE COACHED; A RAZORBACK UNTIL HE DIES

Blytheville's Fred Akers played for the Razorbacks but coached for Texas.

Emcee Larry Lacewell affectionately took caustic note of that a couple of years back at the banquet inducting Akers, among others, to the University of Arkansas Sports Hall of Honor.

Lacewell joked, "I heard someone today here ask Freddie, 'When Arkansas plays Texas again in 2003 and 2004, who will you root for?' And Freddie said, 'Well, you all never fired me.'"

Akers said being voted by the A-Club, the Razorback lettermen, to the Hall of Honor is an incomparable honor.

"A few years ago," Akers said, "I was at the University of Texas and got elected to Arkansas' State Hall of Fame. And I didn't realize at the time that this Hall of Honor would be happening and how much more of a thrill it was to be inducted into this Hall of Honor. I guess it's the fact that it's your peers and teammates, the guys who meant more to you than anything, are asking you to come home and be a part of this family.

"I've been a Longhorn; I've been a Bobcat; I've been a Boilermaker. I've been in national championships and been able to win a couple of them and be involved in 21 bowl games. But I'll tell you, I've never forgotten where my roots are. I've always been a Razorback. And I'll always be a Razorback.

"It doesn't take me long to realize when I come here that I have the same feelings I had when I was a young boy coming to this university. My life has been molded by people here, and some no longer here, all who wished me well and wished me greatness and applauded whether I was or wasn't. That's family. I want to thank all of you for being my family. Family is important. Barry [Switzer, the former Oklahoma coach and Akers's Razorback teammate] and I teed it up for 10 years in a row. But we never forgot one time that with all the competitive drive each of us had we were still teammates, friends and family at this University of Arkansas. We've been bound by that and we will continue to be.

"Your life is not measured by the number of breaths that you take, but rather by the breathless moments that you have and create. And I want to tell you, you have just created another breathless moment for me. I'm very, very proud to be a Razorback."

Gary Anderson

STRONGER THAN HE LOOKED

L ou Holtz is one smart coach, but maybe he out
  smarted himself underestimating Gary Anderson's
toughness.

Holtz never thought the 6'1", 175-pound halfback
from 1979-82 could absorb punishment. So Anderson
gained more than 100 yards on just nine carries when Arkansas opened the 1980 season with a loss at Texas.

Anderson's limited role mystified the man who recruited him out of Columbia, Missouri, former UA receivers coach Jesse Branch.

"Gary won three MVPs in bowl games," Branch said.
"But every year Lou wanted to move him to wide receiver. I
was coaching wide receivers and would have loved to have
had him, but I said, 'Good Lord! We can't move this guy
from running back! He makes it happen at running back.'
He never was hurt. And when he got the ball, he performed
pretty well. I can still see him on that fake reverse when he
scored that first touchdown in 1980 against Texas. He was
flying. Texas has got speed and he's running through them
like crazy. We faked that flanker reverse and he kept it and
scored from like 64 yards out."

COMPARING
ANDERSON AND ALWORTH

B ranch recruited Anderson and was a Razorback
  teammate with Lance Alworth, who went on to
the NFL Hall of Fame as a wide receiver.

Do Anderson and Alworth compare athletically?

"He was a great athlete, as was Lance Alworth," Branch said. "Both could do anything. In speed they were similar. Lance probably had the best hands of anybody I ever saw. He had a knack for catching the ball that was unbelievable. Gary was more of a running back than Lance. I remember he made the darndest touchdown I've ever seen. He dove over from, like, eight yards out. It was on ESPN highlights for two months. Nobody could believe he stayed airborne that long."

Or that he always got up, no matter how big the hit.

"Gary was tougher than nails," Branch asserted.

Anderson looked fragile but obviously wasn't. He endured three years in the USFL while that short-lived league handed out money like candy. He then starred eight years in the NFL with San Diego, Tampa Bay and Detroit and finally spent a year in the Canadian Football League.

How did he last so long as a 175-pound running back?

Think of Kenny Rogers's old song, "The Gambler," and you've got the answer.

"You just had to know when to hold them and when to fold them," Anderson said. "Know when to try and run over somebody and know when to try and run around them. I think people underestimated how strong I was. You've got to know how to run against those big guys [and] when to run underneath."

He still never disputes Holtz's logic about not treating him as a heavy-duty back.

"It did okay for me to get in and out in a hurry," Anderson said. "Let those big backs wear them down. I learned a lot of things on the way with Coach Holtz. Coach Holtz kept me in line. And that helped me a lot in the NFL. I enjoyed him. A coach has to do his job and you've got to respect that. He wouldn't have been coaching as long as he was if he wasn't good at it."

Gary admits some things Holtz did didn't make sense at first.

"I do remember one time I hadn't done anything wrong," Anderson said. "And he was going off on me. We were in a bowl game and he was yelling at me and [fullback] Darryl Bowles to go sit on the sidelines. After we talked to him, he said he hollered because we were getting ready for the game too quickly. He said he was trying to calm us down. A lot of the things he did, you might not know them at the time, but there was a reason for them."

Teddy Barnes

Teddy Barnes

THE IMMORTAL TEDDY BARNES

"The immortal Teddy Barnes" is what Frank Broyles called receiver Teddy Barnes for his surprise route that caught the touchdown pass to open the gates for Arkansas' 31-6 whomping of mighty unbeaten Texas A&M to close the 1975 season in Little Rock.

Barnes's "immortal" catch propelled Arkansas to a piece of the Southwest Conference championship and Broyles's last Cotton Bowl, a 31-10 triumph over Georgia.

"Best that I can recollect," Barnes said 27 years later, "I went deep just to clear it out for Freddie [Douglas, the leading receiver on a team that seldom passed]. I didn't even know to look up for the ball until I saw [A&M All-Southwest Conference defensive backs Lester Hayes and Pat Thomas] running at me."

Actually Teddy and Freddie, "the Katzenjammer Kids," as Broyles used to call his short, hard-blocking receivers from Lepanto and McGehee and their running buddy tight end Marvin Daily of Alma were already immortalized as party animals and the most clever practice players.

"The eye in the sky don't lie," Barnes recalled Broyles and his 1975 offensive coordinator, the late Bo Rein, emphasizing about the film shot from the press box revealing who practiced hard and who didn't. Maybe the eye could get fooled if the three small-town sharpies obtained the right information.

Before each practice one of them always asked film man Dave Patton which portions of practice would be shot and which wouldn't.

So after a particularly hard night of reveling, the trio would go through the motions through the unfilmed portions and then played like Oscar winners for the cameras.

In the late 1990s, Marvin Daily's son Adam joined Houston Nutt's Razorbacks as a fullback whose hard blocking helped Arkansas beat Mississippi State in a key 1999 late-season game at Little Rock and whose career-ending injury in 2000 affected Arkansas severely.

When the Razorbacks were recruiting Adam, Teddy said Marvin confided, "He's not at all like me. They are going to like having him around."

John Barnhill

John Barnhill

TICKETS TO BRAG ABOUT

As Arkansas' athletic director, John Barnhill once discouraged a booster by giving the booster his football tickets.

"He was a man of few words," Nancy Barnhill Trumbo said of her father, Arkansas' football coach from 1946-49 and athletic director from 1946-71. "I remember after he was out of coaching, some man was complaining about his football tickets. Finally, Daddy said, 'Well, take mine then.' The man did, bragging he had seats from the A.D. But when he got to the game, his seats were in the end zone. Being an old line coach, that's where Daddy liked to sit to see the holes open up. The man thought he had been dirty, and Daddy said, 'That's it. I'm out of the ticket business.'"

Chris Bequette

Chris Bequette

EXTRA, EXTRA, READ ALL ABOUT IT

For four of his five years, as a 1983 redshirt for Lou Holtz and letterman for Ken Hatfield from 1984-87, Chris Bequette played offensive guard. He was a smart, effective starter from 1985-87. In '84, though, Chris was a mixed-up reserve defensive tackle, forced to the D-line after a mass exodus of defensive linemen during the Holtz to Hatfield changeover.

Bequette's major duty was replacing rover Nathan Jones as an extra lineman on goal-line stands and short-yardage plays. Chris was literally the extra lineman in the 14-14 season-opening tie against Ole Miss.

"I was in there on five plays," Bequette recalled. "Three of those plays we had 12 men on the field. And it was totally my fault. On the game film, it was so obvious that three plays in a row we had 12 men on the field. Ole Miss was kind of mad at us, but the officials never caught it."

Chris ruefully recalled that he began '84 subbing when he shouldn't have and ended the regular season not subbing when he should.

"The last game of the season against SMU," Bequette recalled of the 31-28 loss, "we go ahead and then they hit a 78-yard pass play. One of those 30-yard passes where the guy is wide open and then keeps going. I thought he would score easy, but he didn't. I was so sure he scored I never heard them call for goal-line defense. I remember Ken Hatfield and [assistant coaches] Fred Goldsmith and Roger Hinshaw all standing around. And Roger Hinshaw turns and says, 'Hey, Chris, aren't you supposed to be in there?'

"SMU lines up, and 190-pound Nate Jones is standing right over one of their 300-pound offensive guards. And Fred [the coordinator] starts dog-cussing me so bad. And Kenny wasn't restraining him. But they didn't check off to Nate Jones's side. They ran to the other side-and scored anyway. But I was distraught. I actually started crying. Afterwards Fred came up and apologized for screaming at me."

CHERICO'S SIGNALS

B equette recalled learning early that undersized redshirt freshman nose guard Tony Cherico in '84 was going to become an all-conference player by hook or by crook.

"Rice is driving on us," Bequette said. "Cherico says, 'Watch this.' They are lining up and Cherico says, 'Hut,' and two of those Rice guys jump off side. Rice knew who did it and they are screaming, but the ref said he didn't hear. They get penalized and it kills their momentum and they don't score."

ONE HOT BUDDHA

B ryan White was a serviceable center that Hatfield inherited in '84. He played well enough to start eventually.

Everyone called him "Buddha" because of his build. Buddha struggled like you would expect a Buddha to struggle in the heat.

"We're playing Rice in '87 in Houston," Bequette recalled. "It had been cool all week in Fayetteville, but it was really hot in Houston and it's so hot on the AstroTurf."

Bequette paused.

"At the end of the third quarter," he said, "we, of course, change ends of the field. It's so hot, but most of us at least do a little jog changing ends. Not Buddha. Buddha has walked the whole way from their 20 to the other 20, and he's picked up a Rice water bottle on the way and he's drinking their water. The referee has respotted the ball and blown his whistle, and Buddha is still 25 yards away, with his helmet off and drinking water. We somehow got the play off, fortunately."

Bequette had one more Buddha story.

"We're playing Texas A&M in 1987," Bequette recalled. "Samuel Bryant, the nose guard, was wearing Buddha out. Buddha was screaming, 'Number 90 is holding me! Hey, ref, number 90 is holding me!' Finally [Razorback offensive tackle] John Stitton and I had enough. We said, 'Buddha, he's on defense. He can hold you.'"

NEVER MIND

Bequette recalled sheepishly his own criticism of teammate Rick Apolskis, a starting offensive tackle, during the 1987 campaign.

"We're out at Texas Tech in '87," Bequette said. "Apolskis hurts his leg and is straddling the sideline. Just a few more inches and they could have pushed him off the field, but no, he's holding up the game for about 10 minutes, and they put it in a cast. So the following Monday we're getting ready for Texas and Rick is practicing. And we're giving him unbelievable hell because he's practicing two days after he holds up the game. We're calling him the Bayer Aspirin Player of the Game. That was the most printable award. Being guys, most of the awards we gave him dealt with feminine hygiene products. He's limping the whole time and we're saying, 'You wuss.' Several weeks go by and they do more X-rays and we found out he really did have a broken leg. So he went from being wimp to the toughest guy."

Eddie Bradford

TWO TOUGH GUYS

Eddie Bradford played for two of the toughest coaches in Arkansas history: Wilson Matthews and Bowden Wyatt.

Bradford's Razorback tenure predated Matthews's legendary UA stay that began as Frank Broyles's right-hand assistant when Broyles became the Head Hog in 1958, but he played for Wilson during Matthews's ultrasuccessful head coaching days at Little Rock Central High School.

At Arkansas, Eddie played two years for easygoing Otis Douglas during an inept 2-8, 5-5 and 2-8 era.

Then came Wyatt, and only the strong survived. In an article for *Hawgs Illustrated*, here's how Bradford described the coaches who commanded instant respect:

"Coach Matthews," Bradford said a year before the death of the UA associate athletic director emeritus, "I haven't graduated yet to calling him Wilson to his face, he meant so much to me as a youngster. He was a very rugged and demanding individual, but also a very caring and loving person. He could be putting his number 12 shoe in your backside at one moment, but before the day was over he'd have his arm around you telling you the facts of life. Playing for Coach Matthews made me a prime candidate to play for Bowden Wyatt, because Coach Matthews and Coach Wyatt were unbelievable disciplinarians."

A disciplinarian, Otis Douglas was not.

"Otis," Bradford recalled of the coach he started every game for in 1952, "didn't take into consideration he was dealing with 17- to 20-year-old kids. He treated kids like they were men and had minimal expectations of them. He was really a wonderful human being, but totally unprepared for the job."

Bradford, at first, wondered if Wyatt was a human being. There were no doubts about the new coach being prepared.

"The day he got here," Bradford said of Wyatt, "and keep in mind I had played regularly as a sophomore, Coach Wyatt said, 'Hey, son, come here, I want to talk to you.' He looked at me and said, 'You are too @#$% fat. If you don't lose weight, I'm going to run you off.'"

Eddie started slimming from 250 to play the next fall at 190.

"That," Bradford recalled of his intro to Wyatt, "was one of the worst shocks I ever had in my life. That whole spring practice I was never above fifth team on the depth chart. It was not only rough physically, but mentally. Those coaches did things then that would bring a lawsuit today. Those guys had a leather strap on their arm, and if you didn't get up as quickly as they would like, they'd pop you on the butt with that thing.

"Coach Wyatt was 38 years old when he got here, but I thought he was 138. I thought it would take that long for a guy to get that mean. There were about 60 guys that disappeared during the course of spring practice. Some of them would leave in the cover of night. I'm not ashamed to tell anybody that I went to bed practically crying every night. You thought it was punishment from the devil himself."

What kept Bradford from fleeing into the night?

"That's a good question," Bradford mused. "Because it was hell on earth. I called my mother one night and said, 'I don't think I can stand it. I'm coming home.'"

He got talked into staying.

"I don't think I could have left anyway," Bradford said. "I couldn't have faced Coach Matthews back home."

Instead he faced up to start every game for a 3-7 1953 team that played all but SWC champion Rice close and molded into the 8-3 SWC champions of '54.

SORRY, MAYOR

Coach Wyatt never let up, even during the most glorious times, like coming back from Austin a 20-7 winner over Texas.

"Coach Wyatt didn't like to fly," former Razorback Eddie Bradford recalled, "so we'd take a bus to Muskogee and then take a train and ride all night to Austin. On the bus back, when we hit the state line from Highway 62 from Lincoln, people were lining the road. I was sitting up at the front of the bus, and we hit Prairie Grove. Some guy, probably the mayor or somebody like that, jumped out and told us to stop. Bowden jumped to the bus driver and said, 'If you stop this damn bus, I'm going to kill you right here! You run over that guy before you stop this bus!' He didn't want us celebrating. He wanted to take us straight to the gymnasium, and he worked our butts off. That was typical for him."

Jesse Branch

Jesse Branch

LEARNING SELECTIVE DISCIPLINE

As a former Razorback player, assistant coach, and associate athletic director, Jesse Branch pretty much saw it all at the University of Arkansas.

One thing he learned from his mentor, Frank Broyles, for whom he played, coached and administrated, was the art of selective discipline.

"We were playing Texas A&M here at homecoming for the conference championship in 1961," Branch said of his Razorback playing days. "We had started going to Eureka Springs at the Crescent Hotel to get away from the crowd. We had a meeting and then we were supposed to go to bed and get a good night's sleep. At breakfast the next morning, there was a whole lot of whispering because after the regular bed check, the coaches had done another bed check.

"They went to this one room where several of our star athletes had a poker game going well after hours. The coaches had knocked on the door and checked the room and found two players all covered up in their beds. Then they started checking the rest of the room and started finding players under the bed, hiding behind the shower curtain—the star athletes. So everybody is wondering what we are going to do. On the bus, Coach Broyles gets up and says, 'I've never been so disappointed! I can't believe we are playing for the conference championship and we have athletes after curfew playing cards! I don't understand it! I don't know what I'm going to do. But there WILL be some disciplinary action taken!'"

Jesse paused. "One of the star athletes hit another star athlete with a halfback pass for the winning touchdown."

JESSE'S VERSION OF
THE IMMORTAL TEDDY BARNES

Frank Broyles called them the Katzenjammer Kids when short, stocky wideouts Freddie Douglas and Teddy Barnes blocked and blocked and blocked and occasionally caught passes on Arkansas' ground-oriented 1975 Southwest Conference tri-championship and Cotton Bowl championship team.

There was one difference between Freddie and Teddy that Branch and offensive coordinator Bo Rein knew well.

"Teddy didn't have very good hands, and Freddie had great hands," Branch said. "So Bo said we always need to have Freddie running that post corner route because we know it's going to be open. I said, 'Bo, I can't do that. They are going to see through that. They've been blocking their little butts off.' So when it was slot right, Freddie was in the slot, and if it was slot left, Teddy was in the slot."

If a pass was slated, it was usually to Freddie's slot.

Except against Texas A&M when the "Immortal Teddy Barnes" caught the touchdown pass from Scott Bull, rocketing underdog Arkansas to a 31-6 stunner over the unbeaten Aggies in December in Little Rock.

"I was the one who signaled in the play that Bo called," Branch said. "It was slot left, and Teddy had gotten in that slot position. Bo is going crazy, and I said, 'Bo, there isn't anything I can do about it now.' The ball is snapped and here they go, and Teddy runs that route between three great defensive backs and goes up and catches it in his facemask for the touchdown. He wasn't supposed to have been in the slot. Freddie was. I said, 'See there. I told you he could do it.' He caught it between Lester Hayes and Pat Thomas, who both went on to be all-pro, and another one who went pro."

DOWN A SLIPPERY SLOPE

Freddie and Teddy were pretty fast in their day, but never faster than on the running slope that Bo Rein suggested and Broyles eagerly constructed during the summer of 1975.

"In the summer," Branch said, "Bo went back to Maryland to talk to their coaches. They had a reputation for speed more than anybody. One of their coaches said how they improved speed was running downhill on a slope. Bo came back and said, 'What they do is get on a 20-percent slope. It makes your feet move faster and it lengthens your stride.' We asked what the slope is, and he says, '20 degrees.'"

Jesse paused.

"Well, Frank gets all excited about it," Branch said. "He gets Bo to get the dimensions and we build this thing– a 40-yard, rubber-surface track going downhill. What happened, though? It was supposed to be a two-degree slope, not 20. They said it would improve your time by three-tenths of a second. Bo and I were down there with Freddie and Teddy to check it out. I started them and they ran all the way down that thing and came out on the other side of the track, and almost snapped their backs. I could see Bo's eyes all the way from the top as he looked at his stopwatch. They had run 3.85! So I saw Coach Broyles, and I said, 'They ran 3.85!' He said, '3.85? There must be something wrong.' I said, 'There is no question something is wrong.'"

No one was ever ordered to run down the slope again. It finally did get some use through several regimes for conditioning running uphill.

"We used to call it Pork Chop Hill," former Razorback tight end Luther Franklin said.

GLUTTON FOR PUNISHMENT

In separate tenures under Frank Broyles and Lou Holtz, Don Breaux established himself as one of the ablest offensive assistant coaches ever to don Arkansas garb.

He's been doing the same thing in the NFL since 1981.

Breaux loved to coach, but he loved at least two things even more: fishing and eating.

"Don Breaux was taking his family to a show at Barnhill one night," Jesse Branch recalled, "and his wife had made a big old batch of cookies. They get to the door at the show and realized they had forgotten their tickets. Don says, 'You wait here. I'll go back home and get the tickets.' He goes back home, gets into the cookies, and comes back and he's forgotten all about the tickets. He still doesn't have them."

Branch reeled off another Breaux tale.

"One time Don was in the dining hall and Coach Broyles called up there from his office and asked him to bring him back a hamburger," Branch recalled. "Don's on his way back down and forgets who he is bringing it for and he ate it."

WELL-TRAVELED COACH

From when he left Arkansas as a player in 1962 until he returned in 1975 as an assistant coach, you'd have needed a road map to keep up with Jesse Branch.

"I played Canadian football for several teams; then I got into coaching and became a vagabond," Branch said. "I coached at Mississippi State and then Kansas State and then the University of Oregon. I didn't even know where that was when I was growing up in Watson Chapel. My wife asked me, 'Where is that?' And I said, 'It's closer to Russia than it is to Arkansas.'"

Oregon might have been closer to Russia, but K-State was football's Siberia back then.

"I spent a couple of years at the University of Oregon," Branch said, "and then went back to K-State. At that time I was the only person in the history of K-State to go back for a second go-round. That was the losingest school in America. I want to thank Coach Broyles for bringing me back here as an assistant in 1975. Then he retired on me in two years and Lou Holtz came in. I coached seven years and five positions under Lou and never got fired. I think I'm the only guy that can say that."

He's probably right.

Russell Brown

Russell Brown

ANTS IN HIS PANTS

Russell Brown said the 1997 Razorbacks' roadtrip to Gainesville was so bad that its start and finish nearly rivaled the middle, a 56-7 loss to the Florida Gators.

Arkansas' 6'0", 290-pound starting left offensive guard from 1995-98 said he never experienced a trip to match it.

"Not only was the trip bad and the game bad," Brown recalled, "but when the plane got to Fayetteville it didn't have stairs. We had to climb a 15-foot stair-step aluminum ladder to get in the plane. Everyone had to climb it. I got an ovation when I made it. And Coach North, he was scared of heights, plus had the stride of about two inches. That was a sight. Coming back home the plane was four hours late. I was laying out on the runway in gym shorts and a shirt and laid on a pile of red ants without knowing it. I was just mad laying down underneath the streetlight. And the next thing I know I'm getting bit everywhere. It definitely put a capper on that trip, the worst I ever had."

That was Brown's worst trip, but not the most hostile setting. Mississippi State fans mobbing the field after their 1998 Bulldogs upset Arkansas, 22-21, in Starkville provided that–although one fan got more than he bargained for.

"I was walking off the field, and two fans jumped on me with those bells," Brown said. "I put my helmet on, thinking I was going to get waxed. I said, 'Guys, get back from me. I'm not in a real good mood here.' One came at me like he was going to hit me, and I said, 'See if you can take this.' I went ahead and hit him a little bit. When I looked up, I didn't know that every media guru in freaking Mississippi saw me wax this guy and knock him out cold."

Did he get in any trouble?

"I got in no trouble," Brown replied. "I went into Coach Nutt and told him, 'I've embarrassed myself and I embarrassed the university and I know it's going to be in every paper tomorrow morning.'

"He asked, 'What did you do?'

"I said, 'A fan jumped on me twice, and I thought he was going to hit me with a bell, so I hit him.'

"He said, 'It sounds like a good case of self-defense to me; get your pads off and let's get started on next week.'

"That's all I heard from him. I got questioned a little bit the next week, but nothing much. I never got any sanctions."

It scared him, though.

"When you bench something like 500 pounds," Brown said, "you forget how big and how strong you are. And when you hit somebody that's normally only playing Nintendo games, bad things happen. That was the scary thing. As a player you are there to have a good time. Saturday is game day."

Until the Starkville experience, Baton Rouge, Louisiana was the most hostile environment Brown recalled.

"LSU is one of the worst places to play. Coach [Virgil] Knight once told us 'Put your helmets on' when we were on the sideline. He said he saw them throwing raw sausage from the upper deck, and sure enough it started coming like bombs from however high they were chunking it. But the SEC is fun. I still miss playing ball bad. I miss it on Saturdays. I miss nothing about it Sunday through Friday, and I sure don't miss spring football."

IS THIS NUTT NUTS?

Russell Brown came out of Bristow, Oklahoma, rough and ready, with an old-school hankering to play for rough and ready coach Danny Ford at Arkansas.

So what was his initial impression as a fifth-year senior starter when crusty, old-school Ford was replaced by bubbly, optimistic Houston Nutt?

The same, he said, as was held by his fifth-year senior starting stablemate, center Grant Garrett.

"When Coach Nutt first came here," Brown said before the 9-3 '98 Hogs played in the Citrus Bowl, "I told Grant, 'I think he'll break out the pom-poms at any time.' I thought, 'Give this time, it's going to wear off.' But his attitude now is even more enthusiastic than when he first talked to us. That's how he is.

"I truly believed we would be successful. We had the athletes. It was just a matter of putting the whole package together, and that's what Coach Nutt was able to do. And the transition really went smooth with Coach [Mike] Markuson [the offensive line coach]. He uses zone blocking, the scheme we were successful with in '95 but got away from. We've developed a relationship with him. The saddest thing about this staff is I won't have a chance to play for them for five years like these guys are going to."

Frank Broyles

Frank Broyles

MY VALUED ASSISTANT

Arkansas Athletic Director Frank Broyles has been known to fumble a name or two, but sometimes he'd just forget them altogether.

During his UA football coaching days from 1958-77, Broyles once was hyping one of those spring football Red-White intrasquad games the Hogs used to play in Little Rock.

They sold tickets to those things then, so with TV mikes on hand the day before the game, Broyles was drawing every rabbit he could out of the hat to hype the game. He even included how the coaching staffs would be divided, right from the coordinators to the graduate assistants. "The Red will have Gordon Norwood and Steve Sprayberry," Broyles said when he got to the G.A.s. "And the White will have Borys Malczycki and...uh...uh...oh...that guy with the glasses..."

DIRTY WORK

During the AstroTurf days of Razorback Stadium, Frank was coaching up in his tower during spring drills. It was one of those noncontact dress rehearsal sessions just before the spring game. It was really informal, with so little going on that one of the players' girlfriends brought her Saint Bernard to the workout.

Nobody cared—until nature called with results that a circus elephant couldn't have produced.

Frank spotted it. Atop his tower, and with the volume of five foghorns, he bellowed, "Manager! Manager! Some dog has just crapped on the AstroTurf!"

Poor Craig Wilson, a UA manager who later worked in Little Rock television before going into private business, was summoned with shovel and bucket to do the dirty work.

OVER THE EDGE

One time during practice, a reserve wide receiver named Kelvin O'Brien caught a pass, ran through the south end zone, and proceeded to heave the ball out of the stadium somewhere towards West Fork.

"My first touchdown as a Razorback," the sophomore explained.

"I believe he has gone crazy," Broyles muttered.

Kelvin figured in one flagrantly wrong call that went the Razorbacks' way at Razorback Stadium against Iowa State in 1973.

Arkansas was running both the slot-I and the wishbone early that season.

O'Brien was in the slot when Broyles substituted a wishbone halfback in a goal-line situation. The only problem was, O'Brien forgot to come out. Arkansas lined up in a 12-man "slotbone." The officials didn't notice, and neither, it seemed, did the Iowa State defense.

Iowa State's defensive coaches in the press box noticed big-time. They couldn't do anything except helplessly squawk on the headset as quarterback Mike Kirkland called a play for the winning touchdown in a 21-19 verdict.

BARBARA'S WAY WITH WORDS

Before moving into the beautiful Baum Stadium, the Razorback baseball team played at George Cole Field.

It was, by far, a cut above Legion Field on the Fairgrounds where the Hogs used to play, but with no lights, George Cole Field was practically outmoded the day it was unveiled in 1975.

So in 1985, former Razorbacks Johnny Ray, Tim Lollar, Kevin McReynolds, and their agent, Tom Selakovich, paid Coach Norm DeBriyn the ultimate compliment by contributing a massive amount of money towards putting in lights.

The lights were unveiled as the Hogs hosted Texas.

It was a packed house, with Frank, his wife Barbara, and an entourage of dignitaries in the press box.

The first pitch to a Razorback was called a strike.

Frank didn't like it. "Strike, noooo!"

He went on that way for several innings. Who was going to tell him he couldn't cheer or boo in the press box? The noise ceased. For quite awhile.

Then that unmistakable Georgia accent returned.

"Forty-five minutes! Forty-five minutes! Forty-five minutes!"

All the yes men nodded, still not knowing 45 minutes of what.

"I had to stand in line for the bathroom for 45 minutes!" Broyles said. "We've got to get those, uh, uh...Barbara, you have a way with words..."

"Port-a-potties, Frank," she said.

Thanks to Barbara's way with words, there were indeed port-a-potties when Arkansas hosted and won the Southwest Conference Tournament a few weeks later.

Also, thanks to Broyles resisting renovation of George Cole Field, the state-of-the-art Baum Stadium was built on an entirely different tract of land that could accommodate all its bells and whistles.

Frank also supervised the state-of-the-art renovation and expansion of Reynolds Razorback Stadium for football, the state-of-the-art construction of Walton Arena for basketball, and the Randal Tyson Indoor Track Center.

BEATS TRAVEL BINGO

The Winged T didn't give Frank Broyles a flying start as Arkansas' new head football coach in 1958, but it did divert Broyles and assistant coach Dixie White on a long, rainy drive to Little Rock.

"We went 0-6," Broyles recalled, "because I got sold on the Winged T and got away from what our team had been successful with at Georgia Tech and Missouri. We junked it after the first game when we made 33 yards against Baylor. I got Dixie White in the car, and driving in the rain to do the TV show in Little Rock I wrote down everything we did offensively in the old belly series. It took us about four games to get all that straight, and we started playing pretty good."

APPRECIATING INSURANCE

"Those first six losses were the first real adversity I had faced in my athletic career," said Broyles, a three-sport star at Georgia Tech, an assistant at Georgia Tech and Baylor and a head coach at Missouri before coming to Arkansas. "When we lost that fifth game, I called my dad and said, 'Save me a place in the insurance company. I'm going to be home quicker than you think.'"

A BETTER POLICY

B royles had a better policy going for him than he realized. Athletic director John Barnhill was absolutely convinced the young coach would take Arkansas to heights never realized.

"All during those games," Broyles said, "Barnie would call Barbara and say, 'Don't worry. Everything is going to be all right. Don't you worry.' At the end of the season, he gave me a raise, extended my contract, and said he had seen Barbara driving an old 1937 Ford. He said, 'Go buy her a beautiful station wagon.' So Barnie bought her our first station wagon. That was really special."

LET'S RERUN OLE MISS

B royles never beat Ole Miss as a coach, but he sure loved his most recent football victory over the Rebels as an athletic director.

Not only did the Razorbacks win in 2001 for the first time at Oxford, Mississippi, but they set an NCAA record with seven overtimes while doing so. The seven OTs made for an instant classic and erased, at least for a while, the continuous delving into the 1969 Shootout that No. 2 Arkansas lost, 15-14, to No. 1 Texas.

"Even though it was a classic and people talk about what a great game it was," Broyles said of he '69 game, "The Mississippi overtime classic is a lot better, because we won."

MELANCHOLY TIMES

B royles starts this 2002 football season more enthusiastic than ever about Houston Nutt and the
Razorbacks but acknowledges there are two holes in his heart
that can't be filled.

For the first time in Broyles's UA tenure, Orville Henry
won't be chronicling the Razorbacks in a newspaper, and
Wilson Matthews, the assistant coach, associate athletic director in charge of the Razorback Foundation and finally
associate athletic director emeritus, won't be watching football practice.

Both icons died last spring.

"Football season will not be the same without reading
Orville and having Wilson around analyzing things for us,"
Broyles said. "They were both phenomenal in their trade."

STILL LIGHTS UP

S till, the Hog calls and the excitement that's so
uniquely Arkansas gets Broyles, 77, acting like a
kid again.

"Houston made a good comment about two weeks
ago," Broyles said in June of 2002. "He had been to about
five Razorback Club meetings, and the spirit, enthusiasm
and passion were at an all-time high. And his quote to me
was, 'It just makes you want to do better and work harder.'
And I told him, 'Now you know what I've felt for these last
45 years.' That's what charges you."

Mike Burlingame

Mike Burlingame

PLAYING THE HEISMAN GAME

Arkansas mounted an injury-curtailed Heisman Trophy campaign for running back Cedric Cobbs in 2000, but it paled to the Heisman Trophy campaign for Razorback center Mike Burlingame in 1979.

"Game," as his teammates called him, was a fifth-year senior starter, though not a stellar one.

"We had a good line in '79 in spite of me," he said.

But he ran such a refreshingly tongue-in-cheek Heisman campaign that he even upstaged coach Lou Holtz, fresh off Holtz's second appearance with Johnny Carson on *The Tonight Show.*

Burlingame said the press guide comments of junior starting offensive tackle Phillip Moon clicked the light to the Heisman campaign.

"Moon said in the press guide that he wanted to be governor of Arkansas," Burlingame said. "Holtz was wanting everybody to have goals. I was from Norman, so I was quite familiar with the Heisman campaign hype from all Oklahoma had. So I told [sports information director] Rick Schaeffer, 'If Moon wants to be governor, I'll run for the Heisman.' That's how all that started."

Schaeffer, now Fellowship of Christian Athletes vice president and administrator but still involved with the Razorbacks as a baseball broadcaster and host of the Razorback Classic retrospective TV programs, remembers it well.

"I'm going in the training room one Sunday to get the injury report from Dean Weber," Schaeffer said. "And Mike Burlingame said, 'Hey, Rick. Who are the leading Heisman

Trophy candidates?' I said, 'Everybody who plays college football is a Heisman Trophy candidate.' He said, 'Well, I want to be a Heisman Trophy candidate.' I said, 'You are kidding.' So then he started rattling off reasons: 'Why shouldn't I be? I touch the ball more than anybody else. I'm never off side.' He had about three or four more good one-liners, and I kept writing them down and it took off from there."

LOU APPROVES

The fact that Holtz supported the campaign was a surprise, considering how serious Lou Holtz was about football and his penchant for having the spotlight on himself and his one-liners.

"The great thing was Coach Holtz," Schaeffer said. "I wasn't sure whether he would think it was very funny. But he did."

Lou even encouraged it.

"We had a lot of freshman on that team," Burlingame said. "He said it took the pressure off. I told him I wouldn't go on Johnny Carson until after the football season, just like him. We had the same priorities on that."

It's a wonder Burlingame didn't get on *The Tonight Show*.

Augmented by the "Hold for Heisman" bumper stickers his teammates had made and mass produced, a ridiculous picture of the 6'2", 250-pound center in the traditional Heisman pose that ran in the *Arkansas Gazette* and the *Arkansas Democrat*, and the "Heisman updates" that Schaeffer inserted into the weekly football game press releases, Game was bombarded with requests for quotes by whimsical columnists everywhere.

GAME AND FARRAH

"I got calls all swinging time," Burlingame said. "One writer from Florida sent me a column that said 'Burlingame has as much chance of winning the Heisman as Farrah Fawcett does of winning an Emmy or an Oscar.' Now she's won one. So I guess I was ahead of my time."

A MID-CAMPAIGN INJURY

Burlingame missed two games in that 10-2 season with a knee injury.

"When he got hurt," Schaeffer recalled, "I asked, 'Is that going to affect your Heisman campaign? And he said, 'Oh, not at all. Now I've got more time to talk to reporters.' After a game, he would say things like, 'I want to thank my backs for hitting the hole when I block for them.'"

Although tackles Greg Kolenda and Phillip Moon and guards George Stewart and Chuck Herman were the stars on the line in '79, the Hogs apparently missed Burlingame. The two games he didn't start, against Houston and in the Sugar Bowl against Alabama, were the 2 of the 10-2.

"I was undefeated as a starter," Burlingame said. "20-0, a plaque I've got says. I just knew which games to start, huh?"

ALL RETURNS NOT IN YET

Did Game get any Heisman votes? "I've heard conflicting reports," Burlingame said. "I know I didn't get invited up there to New York. That's one thing

I'm sure of. I did have some writers say they voted for me. I got one notice that someone did, a writer that wrote me there's too much hype with the Heisman."

So apparently Burlingame didn't challenge Southern California tailback Charles White and Oklahoma halfback Billy Sims.

"I pulled enough votes off Sims to let White win it," Burlingame claims.

Since Burlingame wasn't invited to New York, he had to make his concession speech in Fayetteville.

"The people have spoken," Burlingame said, "...the bastards!"

MR. LUCKY

A subconscious inspiration for Burlingame's Heisman campaign may have been Arthur Lucky, a senior B-team offensive lineman when Mike was a freshman in 1975.

B-team and scout team are polite terms for the players who basically serve as human blocking and tackling dummies simulating the opposing team for the varsity in practice, but the players often called it T-team, for "turd team."

"Arthur Lucky," Burlingame said, "was the one who had a picture painted of himself holding a blocking dummy, and underneath it he had an inscription that said T-Team All-American. He had it hanging in the corner of the staircase."

Since campaigning for the Heisman, Burlingame has gone on to work with young minds. He's taught earth science the past 17 years at Southwest Junior High School in Springdale.

Brandon Burlsworth

EVERYBODY'S ALL-AMERICAN

It wasn't just because he died young and tragically that Brandon Burlsworth is still remembered as everybody's Arkansas All-American.

An unknown, overweight walk-on from Harrison becoming an All-American athletically and academically is a story that lives beyond death.

CLARK KENT WAS SUPER

The car wreck that claimed him shortly after he was drafted by the Indianapolis Colts in the spring of 1999 and the ongoing tributes show that Superman lives on even when Clark Kent dies.

Clark Kent was one of the nicknames that the Razorbacks gave their right offensive guard when he donned Clark Kent-like black frame glasses in his senior year of 1998.

It was the only way Brandon Burlsworth ever made a spectacle of himself. He got glasses strictly to see better with them than he could with contact lenses.

"If I'm on a pull or screen pass," Burlsworth said during a 1998 interview, "I want to be able to see in the secondary. That's why I initially started wearing them. And I got comfortable with them. I got teased a lot. All the time it was Clark Kent or [bespectacled former Los Angeles Laker player and former coach] Kurt Rambis. I don't wear them other than on the field or for driving. I had to get used to them and everybody on the team had to get used to them. It's no big thing."

His teammates loved to kid him.

Once during a practice, starting quarterback Clint Stoerner surprised the huddle when he suddenly had on Burlsworth-type specs as he called the play.

Brandon never dreamed that kids in Arkansas would start wearing his style of eyewear.

"He got those glasses because they were plain," former Arkansas offensive line coach Mike Bender said. "That was Burls. He was unassuming. He didn't want to draw attention to himself."

THE BURLS WAY

In the one year they coached Brandon Burlsworth, Houston Nutt and offensive line coach Mike Markuson quickly learned to love the right guard they called "Burls."

Doing things the "Burls Way" became their slogan after Brandon's death, but it really was their unspoken slogan just after coaching him in spring practice.

THE FORD REGIME GRIEVES

However, it was Danny Ford and his regime that brought Burlsworth to campus. They took the news of Brandon's death hard.

"When [Harrison coach] Tommy Tice called me and told me Brandon had died," Ford said, "I said, 'No way.' I was worthless the rest of the night. I didn't move out of that chair for two and a half hours other than to call his mother. She said, 'Brandon always knew God had his hand on him and he still does.'"

Former Razorback strength coach Virgil Knight, now a construction company owner in Fayetteville, said on the day before the funeral, "I've had two sleepless nights, and I'm a guy who can sleep sitting down."

Ford, Knight, Bender, and former recruiting coordinator Harold Horton, now the vice-president of the Razorback Foundation, all cast huge influences on Burlsworth's career. All say their influence paled to what Brandon accomplished by pulling himself up by his own bootstraps. Brandon was the younger who taught the elders, the elders said.

"He was an inspiration," Bender said. "The reason a man coaches is to come in contact with a Brandon Burlsworth. They come few and far between. It's an honor to be a part of his life."

Ford said Horton is most responsible for Burlsworth being a Razorback.

"We didn't have a clue he could play," Ford said. "He was way overweight. But Harold knew about him and we needed bodies."

Horton said Henderson State and Arkansas Tech had offered Burlsworth scholarships. Arkansas didn't but avidly sought Burlsworth to walk on.

BROTHER KNOWS BEST

Marty Burlsworth, Brandon's older brother whom he made his agent when negotiating with the Indianapolis Colts, accompanied Brandon on his UA visit.

"Marty did the talking," Horton recalled. "Brandon wanted to come here, and Marty wanted to get him a scholarship. We couldn't offer him one. Marty said, 'Well, at the end of the year he will have a scholarship.'"

Brandon did. Ford startled media at his postmortem press conference of the 4-7 '94 campaign by raving about a redshirt freshman scout-team guard named Brandon Burlsworth. The overweight 311-pounder would slim to 252 and then muscle up to a faster, stronger 305.

IF HE AIN'T THE BEST...

"I've never seen a guy come so far," Ford said. "The last time I saw him was after practice [in 1998] at South Carolina. He had that same old smile on his face. And you could always count on him being sad when we got beat. He always had a tear in his eye when we lost. I told somebody, 'If he ain't the best I ever had from top to bottom–Christian young man, student, football player–then he's in the top one percent.' He was so quiet, but whenever he said something, everybody listened."

Bender arrived on Ford's staff in the spring of '95.

"He had lost the weight and was starting to gain some back into muscle," Bender said. "We went inside one day when it was raining and scrimmaged against the defense. We had him at guard, and he was kicking booty. And right there I said, 'This young man is going to be something special.' He was a perfectionist. Everything he did, he did to the best of his ability. He accomplished more in 22 years than most of us will in 75. He prepared for everything–including this. He talked to me so often about his faith."

Credit Knight for the new day of Burlsworth's physique.

"Credit Burlsworth," Knight corrected.

"I can," Knight said, "remember him walking in as a freshman weighing 311, looking like the Pillsbury Doughboy. We said we'd go down in weight until it was best for him at that time. We got down to 252, and then I said we are going back the other way. And he said, 'That means I don't have to eat green labels anymore?' They had the labels for him at the cafeteria on what he could eat. And that's all he ate. He was a man on a mission, and that was to do whatever it took. You'd have to chase him out of the weight room."

Horton recalled one of he most moving tributes to Burlsworth, made by Grant Garrett on a night when Garrett was being honored at a banquet in his hometown of Lake Hamilton.

"Everyone was talking about what a good person, good player and good student Grant Garrett is," Horton said. "And Grant gets up there and says, 'I appreciate all those good compliments. But Brandon Burlsworth–he was a level above me.'"

Bobby Burnett

NO BURNETTS = A LOSING SEASON

Perhaps it's no accident that the 4-5-1 record the 1967 Razorbacks compiled was the lone subpar season Frank Broyles suffered from 1964-70.

It was the only season during that stretch that he didn't have a Burnett.

The Burnett brothers, Bobby, who lettered in 1964 and '65, Tommy in 1965 and '66, and Bill from 1968-70, all had a major impact.

Bobby, the trailblazer and a halfback on the 11-0 national championship team and a 10-1 repeat Southwest Conference championship team, recalled his father's words while being inducted into the UA's Sports Hall of Honor.

"'I never said it would be easy,'" Bobby recalled, "'I said it would be worth it.' That's what my Dad said to me when I finished my career at Arkansas, because I wanted to quit so many times. These coaches were monsters. They yell at me when I'm hurt. I wish I could tell you what Wilson Matthews said to me in practice, but I won't. I've got to keep it clean. But it was worth it. I started out like most everyone does at Arkansas. I played on the T-team. Everybody else called it the scout team, but we called it the T-team. The T was short for, well, the word started with T and ended with D. You can fill it in."

DAMNED IF YOU DO,
DAMNED IF YOU DON'T

The team of the damned might have been more the appropriate title for the T-team.

"I used to have nightmares," Bobby said, "that I would have to run the opponent's plays against the number-one defense. And I knew the only way I could get off this T-team was to make them look bad. That didn't work. Because when I made them look bad, Wilson Matthews would say, 'Run it again.' And all I could say in my dreams was, 'Please don't run it again. I'm getting killed.'

"But these were the greatest five years of my life. I learned about not giving up. I'm so grateful that God gave me the wherewithal and talent to play on that national championship team. I played several years of pro football, but I tell you, the one moment of my career was that one touchdown against Nebraska that gave us the national championship. That was it, guys. From the T-team to the national championship; it can't get any better than that."

Mark Calcagni

GET LOST, MARK

Lou Holtz recruited Mark Calcagni and seldom played him.

Ken Hatfield succeeded Holtz and told Mark Calcagni he ought to forsake playing football and just be a student coach his senior year.

So you wouldn't expect many glowing Calcagni tributes to either coach some 17 years after Mark, now a vice president of sales for J. B. Hunt in Springdale, was a Razorback quarterback.

"My memories of three years with Coach Holtz and two years of Coach Hatfield are good memories," Calcagni said. "I learned from them, and it carries on. I find myself saying to my kids things that Coach Holtz and Coach Hatfield said to us. I liked both of them. It was a different atmosphere with Coach Holtz, a tighter rein. 80 guys were out on that practice field, and all 80 thought that little man was watching him at that very moment. With Coach Hatfield it was loose, not as high-strung mentally where you weren't afraid to make mistakes. Sometimes with Lou, you over-thought. But in the game, he was off you and you were so prepared. It was good to be a part of both styles. It made you more well rounded as a player and a person."

COMPLEXION CHANGE

Quarterbacking for Lou changed Mark Calcagni's complexion.

"There wasn't any pressure in my life like playing for Lou Holtz," Calcagni said. "He was the one who caused my acne. I would be worried about making reads in my sleep."

Ron Calcagni

Ron Calcagni

LOU FINALLY GETS HIS MAN

Quarterback Ron Calcagni was recruited out of Youngstown, Ohio, by both Arkansas head coaches for whom he played.

Obviously, Frank Broyles recruited him, since Ron was a freshman backup in 1975 and the sophomore starter for the athletic director's farewell to coaching in '76.

But Lou Holtz, for whom Calcagni quarterbacked the Hogs to 11-1 and 9-2-1 records in 1977 and '78, recruited him, too.

"I signed a letter of intent with him back at North Carolina State," Calcagni said of when athletes signed conference letters of intent a week before the final, binding national letter of intent. "When he came to Arkansas, Lou remembered that. He said, 'I signed you.'

"Then he told me, 'You aren't tough enough. You can't play for me.' I missed the last part of '76 with a separated shoulder. He knew what made me click. I told him, 'I'm going to show you how tough I am.' The last spring game in Little Rock, I was pretty banged up, both thumbs were banged up, but there was no way I was going to miss. He said, 'As long as you've got your legs, you can make it to the dance.' The quarterbacks we teach now to slide and run out of bounds, he didn't want any of that. He was old-school."

FRANK'S SOUTHERN COMFORT

Holtz was originally from Ohio, just like Calcagni, and had worked for Ohio State coaching legend

Woody Hayes, but Broyles's smooth, Southern style outdid Lou to get Ron to Arkansas.

"Coach Broyles impressed my family with his charm and Southern demeanor," Ron said. "My younger brother Mark made the comment that Coach Broyles was bigger than Woody Hayes. He was impressed." So impressed that Mark joined Broyles and Holtz and signed with Arkansas as a quarterback in 1981.

"Frank Broyles closed the deal," Ron said. "But Bo Rein had it wrapped up."

Another irony.

Rein, Arkansas' offensive coordinator for the Southwest Conference championship season of 1975, had been Holtz's offensive coordinator at North Carolina State in '74. He left Arkansas to succeed Holtz as North Carolina State's head coach in '76 when Holtz left for his lone NFL coaching stint with the New York Jets.

Rein later became head coach at LSU and perished in a plane crash on a recruiting trip.

WHAT HAPPENED IN '76?

Arkansas went 10-2 and won the Cotton Bowl in '75, and the '77 team went 11-1 and won the Orange Bowl.

So what happened to a 1976 team that the NFL draft indicates might have been more talented than either squad yet went 5-5-1?

"We had so much talent," Calcagni said, "but we just didn't have a quarterback. I'm teasing there, but I was young. Before that season started, Coach Broyles said, 'You've got a lot of good players around you. Use them. You're just a sophomore; you don't have to be hero.' But it was a tough road and I had injuries. What hurt me the most was that last game against Texas. I couldn't line up. It broke my heart. We knew it was Coach Broyles's last game."

DO BE A HERO

Only once, Calcagni recalled, did a coach ask him to be a hero.

That was before the epic 31-6 Orange Bowl upset of Oklahoma when Holtz had suspended top running backs Ben Cowins and Micheal Forrest and top wide receiver Donny Bobo for disciplinary reasons.

"Probably the greatest upset in college football," Calcagni said. "Coach Holtz called me and said 75 percent of our offense was going to be gone. And he said, 'Ron, you and I are going to win this ballgame. The first four plays of the game, no one else is going to touch the ball, and you are going to score the first touchdown.' I was really surprised, because all year he had said nothing but things like 'there is no I in team.' But he had a plan."

The plan was to make sure there would be no Arkansas turnovers in the early going, keep it in Calcagni's hands, and let Roland Sales, suddenly promoted from third-team to first-team, get his feet wet at running back.

Sales's feet not only got wet, but he achieved 205 yards rushing.

"Guys made their blocks and got a hat on a hat," Sales said. "And Roland had to make Zack Henderson, their free safety, miss, which he did. After that conversation, I believed in our system and we believed in one another, and we were so prepared. Confidence comes with knowing your assignments. Coach Holtz always said that, and it was true."

Earl Campbell

THE TYLER ROSE BLOOMS OVER ARKANSAS

From 1974-77, eventual NFL Hall of Fame Texas running back Earl Campbell helped beat Arkansas every year.

In 1974, Campbell didn't need to run the ball to beat the Hogs. He beat them blocking a punt.

Former Arkansas offensive lineman Allen Petray remembers well, too well, when Frank Broyles ordered the Hogs to run out the clock with the game close just before the half at Austin.

"I was in the game," Petray said. "We were behind a touchdown or so, had the ball on our own 20 or something like that, maybe a minute and a half left and Frank calls handoffs down the middle."

Petray paused.

"We're wondering, 'What the...?'" he recalled, noting Texas called time. "It's something like fourth and five, we line up for a punt. Doug English is my assignment. A punt rush was on. I was the guard; Bruce Mitchell, God bless his soul, was the upback. I remember seeing a shadow move. I glance back before the snap and no upback. Bruce shifted to the strong side. Texas was using the old 'swinging gate' punt block formation. Soon as I turn back, a player jumps in the gap between center and me and the ball is snapped. I remember a flood of orange jerseys then a double thud. I ran back knowing the punt was blocked and see Doug English grabbing the ball in the endzone for a touchdown. Mind you, this was on national television."

Of course there was hell to pay.

"Mervin Johnson [the offensive line coach] was tearing my ass up in the dressing room at halftime," Petray said. "It wasn't until next day that the film showed what happened. The man that jumped in the gap was Earl Campbell, and he blocked the punt. Funny thing, but looking at the film, I was even with Doug English grabbing for the ball, but I don't remember it. I was in a panic at the time. I might have gotten to the ball for a safety. Then we would have gotten beat by four and a quarter touchdowns instead of five."

Texas won 38-7.

NO MORE HIGHLIGHTS, PLEASE

Earl Campbell still ranks among the nicest of guys ever to play football, but former Arkansas safety Tommy Harris fervently hopes being elected to the Pro Football Hall of Fame was the last honor for the Tyler Rose.

"Every time Earl gets honored," Harris said, "they show highlights. And every time they show highlights they show me. Our nose guard, Wayman Hawkins, does some kind of stunt and runs the wrong way. No nose guard. The center must have taken out a linebacker, because I'm left with Earl and he's got a full head of steam."

Did Tommy, a rangy 185-pounder, pull a discretion-is-the-better-part-of-valor matador swipe and fall or did he take on the 240-pounder with sprinter's speed and freight train power?

"No," Harris replied. "Like a fool, I took him on. It was like roadkill. He ran right over me, flattened me right on the AstroTurf. Every time he'd get an award, they'd show it. It was like, 'Here we go again.'"

Ronnie Caveness

CAVENESS INCITES WILSON'S WRATH

Ronnie Caveness earned first-team All-American honors, was named to the Razorbacks' All-Century team and was an inductee in the University of Arkansas Sports Hall of Honor.

All those feats may be secondary to a feat he almost accomplished lettering as a linebacker for Frank Broyles's Razorbacks from 1962-64.

Caveness almost made it through Arkansas with his mental backside unscathed from a Wilson Matthews tongue-lashing.

Wilson, the recently deceased associate athletic director emeritus, has long been legendary as a hide-blistering motivator and disciplinarian serving as Broyles's right-hand man as a linebacker coach, administrator, and before that, as the state's most successful high school head coach ever while coaching at Little Rock Central.

"He was the smartest coach I ever played for," Caveness said of Matthews prior to the Hall of Honor ceremonies. "He knew exactly what the other guys were going to do, and he had a strategy. And a great motivator. Everyone talks about Coach chewing somebody out; all I got were pats on the back."

Amend that. Almost all he got were pats on the back. Ronnie figures he may have gotten one of Wilson's most public figurative kicks in the backside of any Razorback ever. That kick might have become literal had Wilson not needed Ronnie so badly.

It came during the Hogs' national championship 10-0 season of 1964 in the 14-13 victory over Texas in Austin. Texas was about to try a do-or-die two-point conversion.

"I look over there to get the signal," Caveness recalled, "and Coach Matthews threw up that signal and I said, 'Man, there's no way we're running this thing.' He lined us up in a pass defense and we're close to the goal line. I didn't see it, but Texas had taken [halfback Ernie] Koy out of the game and put in a receiver.

"So Coach factored that, but I thought, 'No way, I'm going to call timeout. I'm going to the sideline and get this thing straightened out.' The moment they called timeout, here comes Coach on the field. That cleared up everything. I knew exactly what he wanted. He was ready to get right into me. I called that defense and the linebackers went out over the defensive tackles. The middle was wide open. If the quarterback had looked at it he could have walked three steps and been in the end zone. But the quarterback never saw it. He just hummed their signals and tried the play they called."

And Arkansas stopped it en route to both a Southwest Conference championship and the Football Writers' Grantland Rice national championship trophy after a 10-7 Cotton Bowl victory over one of Bob Devaney's mighty Nebraska teams.

"I was in New York for an awards deal with Tommy Nobis," Caveness said of the Texas All-American linebacking great who also played on the offensive line at times. "They had put him in at offensive guard on that last drive, and he said, 'That was pretty smart of you all to get in that pass defense.' I said, 'Yeah, we worked on that a lot.' It did work out."

The more Caveness thought about it, the more he recalled that maybe that wasn't the first time that Matthews had set him straight.

But Wilson always salved what he blistered.

"I never left the practice field, even though we went through some butt-chewings," Caveness said, "without Coach coming up at the end of the day saying, 'Forget about today. We've got tomorrow.' He always left you with something positive. He never told you what you should do or you shouldn't do. He always left that up to you. He gave you a confidence."

SHUCKING NEBRASKA

Caveness said the Hogs needed all the confidence they could muster when they first eyed Nebraska, a program ahead of its time in weight training.

"A tough, tough, football team," Caveness said of the Cornhuskers. "They were the first physically big football team. Nobody we played came close to their size. They had just started their weightlifting program, and they were big and fast. We were skinny guys. If you looked at it on paper, there was no way we should have been able to compete. But you look back on our '64 team; we had more heart than ability. Everybody played a role. There were no superstars–just a bunch of guys coming together and getting after it. In the fourth quarter, our opponents were still figuring out why we were still in the game–especially Nebraska, because they had tremendous size.

"Their running back named Wilson weighed 225 pounds. Our defensive tackle weighed that. Their offensive line was 240, 250; that was kind of unheard of in those days. That game was kind of the epitome of our season. We had a good game plan and we were able to make an 80-yard drive in the fourth quarter. [Quarterback] Freddy Marshall had key plays throughout that drive, and Bobby Burnett scored the touchdown."

Caveness asserted that the fans in the stands willed that victory.

"I always said after the time we played Nebraska, it was the Razorback fans, 10, the Nebraska fans, 7," Caveness said. "Those fans were unbelievable. We had to go 80 yards in the fourth quarter, and the fans did it for us. They came to their feet, the whole drive. And when Burnett came into the air, it looked like he had wings getting across that goal line. I still have that video in my brain. The crowd went nuts. It was something I'll always remember. Nebraska had great fans, dedicated fans, but they didn't match up to ours. The Razorback fans came through."

A HURRICANE BLOWS IT

The other game that stood out to Caveness might surprise you. Tulsa seldom gets a second thought by Razorback fans anymore. TU was a team the Hogs beat regularly when the Hurricane used to dot the UA schedule. But the 1964 Hurricane team, with quarterback Jerry Rhome and receiver Howard Twilley, had cause to think it could blow past the Hogs. That cause looked ripe to succeed with an early TU lead.

"Rhome was a super, super quarterback," Caveness said. "And their coaches wanted to beat Arkansas so bad. And they were up on us, 14-0, before you could turn around. They had Howard Twilley, an excellent receiver, and they played with a pro concept. But they had an option play with the halfback, and he got mixed up and threw one of those duck-flying-in-the-air type passes, and I intercepted it and took it in. And then I recovered a fumble, and we were only down 14-10 and went on to win [31-22]. Rhome was telling me that the halfback who threw that pass never played again the entire year. That's how bad they wanted to beat Arkansas. They had a good football team; they went on to beat Ole Miss in the Bluebonnet Bowl."

Caveness believes Arkansas' success of 1964 is owed to its failures of 1963. After going 9-2, 8-3, 8-3 and 9-2 from 1959-62, Broyles's Hogs dipped to 5-5 in '63.

"That's one of the strangest things about football," Caveness said, "you learn more when you lose. So we learned a lot in 1963. That was a senior-loaded football team, something like 23 seniors, and went 5-5. And so we went to work. One of the biggest things we had learned is you can't cut corners. You've got to go to work and sweat and play fundamental football and believe in each other. The leadership from our 15 seniors; we had to get that. And the coaching staff learned, too. They rededicated themselves."

Tony Cherico

Tony Cherico

CHERICO GETS CANNED

Tony Cherico had started 15 straight games when Ken Hatfield canned him. Or when Cherico and J.R. Brown canned themselves.

Hatfield's social call to their Wilson Sharp Dormitory took an unsociable turn for starting sophomore nose guard Cherico and reserve halfback Brown and left them home the following Saturday while Arkansas won its 1985 Southwest Conference opener, 41-0, over TCU in Fort Worth.

"Coach Hatfield was just visiting people in the dorm after eating lunch at the cafeteria," Cherico, now a high school football coach in Dallas, said. "I was in class, and J. R. was in the room. Coach Hatfield noticed some beer cans on the floor. He said we needed to see him immediately."

Immediately meant putting football ahead of academics.

"J. R. got me out of class," Cherico said. "I couldn't believe what it was for. Coach Hatfield said, 'You are going to be second team at practice today, and then we'll let you know what is going to happen.' That night he told us we'd be on the scout team all week and wouldn't play in the game."

No road trip because of empty beer cans?

"We couldn't believe it," Cherico said. "TCU was a big game for us because they had scored 17 points in the fourth quarter to beat us the year before, and we really had something to prove. But I tell you something, after getting into coaching, I really appreciated what that man did. Rules are rules, and they are supposed to be followed. He held you accountable whether you were a walk-on or a starter."

A HATFIELD BELIEVER

Cherico signed out of Kansas City with Lou Holtz's Razorbacks in 1983 and redshirted when Hatfield replaced the fired Holtz after the '83 season.

And while some of his teammates preferred Holtz's more lax rules on how they spent their free time to Hatfield's stricter approach, Cherico preferred the new coach's quieter approach to practice and discipline to Holtz's legendary sharp-tounged temper.

"I was scared of that little man," Cherico said of Holtz. "Everybody was. He intimidated you. He did the magic tricks and all that, but that year as the season went on he got real withdrawn. Now Coach Hatfield had recruited me for Air Force, so I knew him and I was excited. I knew he believed in me and that players my size could play because that's what he mostly had to play with at Air Force."

GHOST OF TEXAS PAST

His last Arkansas-Texas game still haunts Cherico. Arkansas led Texas the whole game in 1987 at Little Rock until the last play, a Texas touchdown pass that won it 16-14.

"I've never heard," Cherico recalled, " a stadium that loud get so quiet so fast."

Steve Conley

ON THE RIGHT TRACK

Steve Conley was a bigger track guy than his brother. And there was no bigger track athlete in the Razorbacks' history than Mike Conley, an Olympic gold and silver medalist in the triple jump, a nine-time NCAA long jump and triple jump champion, and the NCAA outdoor 200-meter dash runner-up the only the time he ran it at nationals.

But Steve Conley was a bigger jumper.

"I got too big to triple jump," Steve, 6'6", said, "and then I got too big to long jump, too. One time I was long jumping and I hit the board and I broke it. I said, 'I'm fixing to be a football player. I'm done with track.' I weighed 175 when I got here and weighed 227 when I left. Right now I go 245."

Steve was never known as Mike Conley's fat little brother, by the way.

The football walk-on, after first dabbling in Razorback basketball and track, became an All-SEC defensive end in 1995 and a third-round draft choice of the Pittsburgh Steelers.

Conley played several years in the NFL, one year in Canada, and even played in the XFL before returning to the UA to finish his degree in 2002.

What was it like in wrestling promoter Vince McMahon's XFL, where the cheerleaders were nearly rated X and the sideline announcers did everything but interject their own strategies into the huddle?

"Now the cheerleaders," Conley said, "and the announcers coming up to you during the game, that was different. But the rest was just football."

Football, with on-the-spot media criticism.

"You'd just make a bad play," Conley said, "and a guy would stick a microphone in your face and say, 'How did it feel to get beat for an 80-yard touchdown?' I had a situation where I did a dash for the ball in the Birmingham game. I was beating the guy to it and I just slipped and fell, and it was on NBC and everybody back home was watching it. The guy asked me about it and I just gave him a look. But the money was legit, and they were paying me good."

Football carved Steve a niche in the family tree that branched off after always being next in line to older brother Mike's track and basketball exploits at Chicago Lutheran High School.

"I always did exactly the same thing he did in high school and college," Steve said. "But where we separated was football. That's when I became Steve Conley as opposed to Mike Conley's little brother. I never was upset to be Mike Conley's little brother. He's a great athlete, one of the best ever at his sport, so that's a compliment. But I ended up making a name for myself."

Steve Cox

Steve Cox

ZORRO

No swords were involved, but Steve Cox can say he played in *The Mark of Zorro.*

In fact, the former Razorback placekicker and punter from Charleston, Arkansas, made Zorro his mark while kicking off in Little Rock against the Texas Tech Red Raiders.

"The Red Raider was behind the goalpost," Cox recalled. "And my kickoff hit the horse in the rear. Zorro raised up...I don't think he fell off, but it was a bull's eye. [Former Razorback] Kim Dameron called me up one time laughing, 'Remember when you hit the horse?'"

IF YOU CAN BEAT 'EM, JOIN 'EM

Former All-Southwest Conference punter and long time NFL kicker Cox had a lot of kicks that made Razorback fans smile.

He's most remembered, though, for three field goals that made them cry. As a University of Tulsa freshman in 1976, Cox kicked three field goals in a 9-3 TU victory at Razorback Stadium over Frank Broyles's last Razorback team.

"I told someone the other day," Cox said a couple of years ago, "that when people talk about Steve Cox it's when I played for Tulsa and we came over in 1976 and won, 9-3. I can't shake that memory. We had a heck of a defense that year at Tulsa. There were quite a few Arkansas boys on that team. Ronnie Hickerson, our quarterback, was from Texarkana. Jerry Taylor, a wide receiver, was from Fort Smith.

DeWalden Frazier and Dell Oliver were from Pine Bluff. They played a big role in that game; all those guys did."

None bigger than Cox, though. Did he catch much flak coming home to holiday in Arkansas after beating the Razorbacks?

"Everywhere I went," Cox replied. "But kickers are used to catching flak. It was a compliment that they were on me."

Certainly everyone in Arkansas hailed him for his 1979 and '80 Razorback seasons after redshirting upon transferring from Tulsa in 1978.

"God, I loved playing for Arkansas." Cox said. "There's not a better feeling than kicking at an Arkansas game in warmups and then running through that 'A'. I wanted to go to Arkansas all along. My sister was a majorette here. And we came to every Razorback game in Little Rock and Fayetteville, sat in the end zone every week. I'd sit there and watch Bill McClard and Tommy Cheyne kick every week. In my 10th grade year, they signed Steve Little. And I knew then, I probably needed to start looking for another place to go. He was such a great kicker. They were high on him and deservedly so."

Cox outdueled Little in that 9-3 game, but Little hit one for the record books.

"That day in Fayetteville when we beat them 9-3," Cox said, "I watched that guy kick a 61-yard field goal. He trotted off the field, and I said, 'He really is as great as they say.' Then he had tough luck from there on out. But I tell you, he was a great kicker. And the Southwest Conference was full of them, with Little, [Texas A&M's] Tony Franklin and [Texas's] Russell Erxleben."

Mike Cross

CROSSING FROM FOOTBALL TO MEDICINE

Mike Cross walked on from DeWitt as a Razorback football player and walked through UA graduation to become a doctor instead of requiring one.

That was no small accomplishment playing for demanding defensive backfield coach Bob Cope on Lou Holtz's staff in the 1970s.

"Bob Cope was my coach, and he was mean," Cross said. "He used to grab my face mask and shake it. He'd say stuff like, 'My little daughter can do better than that!' And I'd think, 'Thanks, Coach. A few years of therapy and maybe I'll recover from this moment.'"

Sometimes it took smelling salts to recover.

"Man," Cross said, "I got knocked out I don't know how many times. But Kirk Woolfolk got knocked out more than anyone. I remember we used to spear people. We were taught to plant your head in there. 'Make 'em pee blood.' That's what Coach Cope wanted. It was fairly aggressive, but it was fun."

Now, Cross takes out his aggression on breast cancer as an oncologist in Fayetteville.

BAD TIMING

A scout-teamer making a big hit on a starting quarterback can expect one of two drastically different reactions.

"I remember," Cross said, "John Scott knocked out [starting quarterback Ron] Calcagni in an early December practice and went to the Orange Bowl because of that. Of course, I remember doing that to [quarterback] Tom Jones one time and Lou chewed me out. It's like, 'What do you want me to do? Stand there and get run over?'"

Yes, usually.

"I remember I had to hold a dummy for Dan Hampton, and he rolled me," Cross said. "Those guys were mean. They had an attitude. That's why they did so well."

Hampton, the Razorbacks' All-American defensive tackle who became an NFL Hall of Famer with the Chicago Bears, and Cross were roommates.

They were an odd couple—the thin, walk-on, doctor-to-be and the carefree ruffian.

"Dan and I had one class together, and we made the same grade," Cross said. "I went and he didn't."

Of course Hampton was no dummy. And he had talents other than football.

"He was so talented musically," Cross said. "You could put any record on and he could play it on his guitar. Incredibly talented musically."

THE REAL INTIMIDATOR

Hampton was big and strong, but nobody intimidated Razorback teammates in the 1970s like offensive guard Mark Lewis.

"I remember Mark Lewis shaving my head when I was a freshman," Cross said. "He scared me to death. Seniors ruled then. They shaved all our heads when we lived in the dorm. I heard he was at Steve Little's funeral and was like a big teddy bear, real cordial. But man, everyone was scared of him. He looked like Charles Manson."

Chuck Dicus

WAVING THE WHITE FLAG

Razorback two-time All-American wide receiver and current Razorback Foundation President Chuck Dicus never had to be carried off the football field until the day after he was enshrined into the College Football Hall of Fame.

"The day after the inductees are enshrined," Dicus said, "they hold a clinic for kids with the enshrinees teaching them how to run routes and run the ball and block. After that, they have a flag football game. They divide the enshrinees up and we act like we are young kids all over again."

Including the playground rules of the biggest demanding the best assignments.

"This day it was two five-man teams," Dicus said. "Willie Lanier, the great linebacker who played for the Chiefs, was on our team. We got in the huddle and Willie said he wanted to be quarterback. I certainly was not going to argue with him, though I was kind of looking forward to doing that myself. But I said, 'Let's go for it and try and score on the first play.' We ran a route and he threw it and I caught it for the first touchdown of the day. I was feeling pretty good and thinking this will be a lot easier than I thought.

"We had played for about 15 minutes and I was on defense. As I was backpedaling to cover someone, I turned on my leg and it felt like someone had thrown the football and hit me right on my ankle. I fell to the ground, and as soon as I rolled over, I knew exactly what had happened. The Achilles [tendon] had snapped. It was pretty embarrassing. There were 300 or more [people] watching this, including my family. They had to carry me off to the sideline and then get a wheelchair to get me to the ambulance. My pride was damaged greatly. But at least I made Arkansans proud by scoring the first touchdown."

He hasn't scored one since.

"I can tell anyone," Dicus said, "that the Achilles is not something you want to mess with. It will never be the same, but it's good enough for me to do what I want to do. I'm not going to be playing any more flag football. Golf and fishing is all I do, and it's good enough for that."

HEAVING A SIGH OF RELIEF

Dicus was so nervous as a sophomore rookie opening the 1968 season that he didn't know if he could stomach it.

Then he decided he could, smiling, because he saw a veteran teammate couldn't stomach it—and not because of nerves.

"Bruce Maxwell was a great player," Dicus said of the Arkansas fullback, "but he was also known for not adhering to training rules. I'm not sure Bruce ever made All-Southwest Conference. But he may have made All-Dickson Street."

Dickson is the street near campus with the most watering holes.

"He was well known at Maxine's Taproom and a lot of other places. I can remember when we took the field against Oklahoma State in 1968 for the opening game in Little Rock. I was a sophomore and really nervous. And in the huddle for our first three or four series, Bruce had the dry heaves. It was so funny to me. I kind of laughed my way through the first quarter. Bill [Montgomery] was calling plays in the huddle and everyone was snickering because Bruce had the dry heaves. But he was a great football player."

Danny Ford

Danny Ford

DANNY'S ENGLISH

D anny Ford presented an intellectual dichotomy. No Razorback football coach ever worked harder to get his Hogs to go to class. Yet nobody ever fractured the English language on a daily basis more than the shrewd Alabama farmer who coached Clemson to a national championship in 1981 and rebuilt Razorback recruiting and team discipline (though he coached only one winning UA year in five).

Asked about a player who was presumed about to be flunking out, Ford replied, "Well, he ain't no scientific rocket."

When one of his Razorback teams played a weak first half and then surged to a close-but-no-cigar finish in the second half, Ford remarked, "We're like Hekyll and Jyde."

Danny could string together so many double negatives that it was no wonder his Hogs once got a delay of game penalty coming out of a timeout.

All those "nots" tied them in knots, it seemed.

Before one of the annual August preseason conditioning tests, Danny was heard to exhort his team: "Don't not nobody not not make it."

Say what?

Danny got so conscious of his grammatical gaffes that he sometimes corrected corrections originally correct.

Greeting a surprisingly large crowd on the Fan Appreciation Day he initiated to allow fans to meet the Razorbacks in preseason, Ford said, "I'm pleased that you all have come here–I mean have came."

EVEN A SAINT CAN'T GO HOME AGAIN

Saint Nelson, an ex-Marine walk-on who helped the Hogs strictly as a practice player went through Senior Day in 1996. He got to run through the "A" at Razorback Stadium and be announced pregame like all the other seniors.

Then it was discovered that because of a clerical error, he actually had another year of eligibility. So Saint came back the next year, helping again as a scout-teamer in practice.

Would Saint go through Senior Day again, Ford was asked before the final 1997 Razorback Stadium game?

"No," Ford replied. "I asked him, but he's got a job on weekends and don't want to go through it anyhow. Kind of a been that, done there."

PUTTING GOLF OUT TO PASTURE

When Frank Broyles hired Danny Ford to be the head coach, it definitely did not include Ford being Frank's golfing buddy.

As the press conference announcing Ford's hiring as Head Hog began winding down, a reporter said, "Well, now on to the important things–GOLF!!!"

The reporter then jiggled into a pantomime stance and swung.

"Golf!" Ford sneered. "That's just a waste of good pasture land."

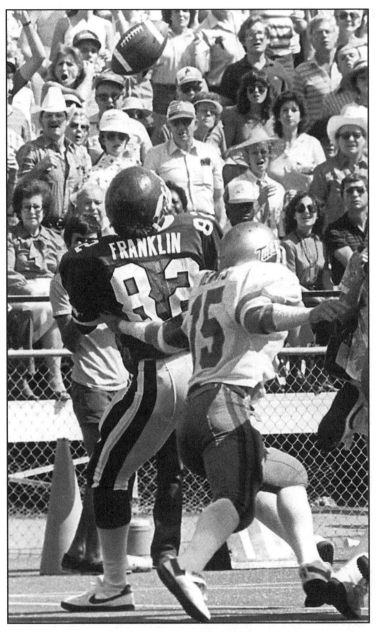

Luther Franklin

Luther Franklin

LUTHER VOTES FOR LOU

Some Razorbacks who played for both Lou Holtz and Ken Hatfield liked Ken better and some liked Lou.

Luther Franklin was a Lou fan, though he admits playing for Holtz provided some exhilarating highs and some way-down lows.

The tight end, who lettered from 1982-85, learned of the ups and downs early–when Holtz came down to Houston to recruit him.

"Lou came down twice," Franklin said. "The principal's mom was from Arkansas and a big Lou Holtz fan. He talked to the principal's mom for an hour. And he came by the house twice. The second time I knew he was coming. I called about 30 people. It was like a party, and he wasn't too happy about that. He said, 'When we're down here recruiting, we mean business.'"

Lou could, and presumably still can, considering the turnaround he's achieved at South Carolina, motivate via a joke or a snarl and all things in between or beyond.

"He could make you feel like you could pick up a telephone and hit a baseball with it," Franklin said. "He made you feel like you could do anything. He could motivate. When he built you up, he built you up. But I also remember in practice we were running a two-minute drill and I ran the wrong play. He grabbed my facemask and my face went over here, over here and over here. I had to put ice on my neck after practice. I almost went home that day. I wasn't used to anything like that. He had a temper on him. If he told you something, he expected you to learn it. But when he left, I thought of transferring."

DIDN'T HIT IT OFF

"The whole deal with me and [Coach] Hatfield," Franklin said, "was getting off on the wrong foot the very first day he was here. I didn't know anything about him, didn't know what he looked like and never met him. We are all sitting there in a room and just talking. I have my back to the door and I'm just BS-ing with the players. He walks in and says, 'When I walk in, you should all be quiet and stand at attention.' And I was like, 'Well, who the hell are you?' And he said, 'I am your head coach.' I apologized and said, 'I didn't know. I didn't know you were the head coach. You didn't announce yourself.' But there was bad blood from then on. That first meeting was it."

FRANKLIN BAFFLES BEARS

Franklin did figure prominently in a big victory over Baylor. He caught a surprise touchdown pass. Any pass to the tight end was a surprise in Hatfield's run-oriented wishbone offense that used wideout James Shibest as the chief receiving threat.

Baylor covered everybody but Franklin, it seemed, as he caught Greg Thomas's pass for a 50-yard TD with 6:09 left, leading to a 20-14 victory.

"It was a big surprise," Franklin said. "I was sitting over there when [tight end coach] Ken Turner was saying, 'Throw the ball to Luther. They won't expect anybody to throw the ball to Luther. Throw it to Luther. It will catch them off guard.' He was saying that to Hatfield. There were a lot of things going through my mind. But I caught it and did my little touchdown thing, but when they wanted to shake my hand I just said, 'Thanks' and did nothing else because I didn't appreciate what they were saying."

Well, it was the truth about him being an unexpected receiver.

"Well, yeah," Franklin said, "he was right about that. I was wide open. They did a little fullback fake dive and I act like I'm going to do a little stalk block on the cornerback and he takes off and bites on the run. And Greg Thomas pulled up and threw it to me. I think the play was called 117."

The 215-pounder, minute for a tight end, sprang another surprise against Texas A&M, though it went mostly unnoticed. "Other than the Baylor game," Franklin said, "the game I remember most is when we played A&M, and [future All-NFL defensive end] Ray Childress came up after the game and patted me on the back and said, 'You are one hell of a blocker.' I said, 'Why do you say that?' And he said, 'Because my coach told me I ought to have 20 sacks this game because Arkansas has this little bitty tight end that you should dominate and throw around like a rag doll. But you are one good blocker.'"

Reggie Freeman

Reggie Freeman

REGGIE'S LOTT IN LIFE

Arkansas stood as much of a chance of beating Oklahoma in the 1978 Orange Bowl as little Razorback nose guard Reggie Freeman stood of slowing down the Sooners' fearsome wisbhone offense.

Well, Lou Holtz's Hogs won, 31-6. And fifth-year senior Freeman so bedeviled touted OU quarterback Thomas Lott with Monte Kiffin's coordinated defense that Freeman was named the Orange Bowl Defensive Player of the Game.

"I was only 206 pounds," Freeman, now an assistant high school principal, recalled. "They must have thought, 'He's just a little bitty ant. He's not going to do anything to us.' But Monte Kiffin changed me around. Instead of playing me straight up over the center, he let me play outside of the tackle. My job that night was as soon as the ball was snapped, just go uphill. And wherever Thomas Lott was, I had to follow him. If he went up to the stands, follow him. If he goes to the bathroom, follow him. Wherever he went, I had to follow."

He must have followed Lott like a shadow.

"Yes, I did," Freeman said. "And that was great. I had six quarterback sacks. I think they went into the game thinking Arkansas had a high school team instead of a college team with. They took us for granted. They were the Oklahoma Sooners, the No. 1 offensive team in the country. And we were just the little bitty Razorback team. That was a raging defense, five, six, seven guys around the football, running, screaming to the ball. Everybody contributed. And you couldn't beat that."

Jim Grizzle

GRIZZLED STEAK

Few ever came to the University of Arkansas more shrewdly naive than Jim Grizzle, out of Fort Smith, joining Frank Broyles's Razorbacks in 1960.

"When I signed with the Razorbacks," Grizzle said, "it was the first time I ever went out to eat.

"The waitress said, 'How do you want your steak?'

"I said, 'I just want the meat.'

"She said, 'How do you want your dressing?'

"I said, 'I want it all.'

"I got the highest price steak. But after I signed they forgot about me. They were courting this kid from El Dorado. We went to the high school all-star game and for TV and the papers they asked, 'Where are you going to school?' And I said, 'Really, I'm undecided.' We started practicing and I saw these long legs running across the field. It was Coach Broyles. He said, 'Jimmy! Jimmy! What do you mean?'

"I said, 'You've been hustling this guy all week with steaks and I've just been getting sandwiches. I want some good stuff to eat.'"

GRIZZLE'S DRINKING PROBLEM

A drinking problem back in 1963 could have drained the business, though Grizzle never drank.

"At the Sugar Bowl after the ballgame," Grizzle said of the 1962 Hogs' New Year's Day loss to Ole Miss, "they let us charge stuff to the room. I charged turtle soup. It was green. It looked awful. I never ate any of it, but I charged it because it was high."

Not as high as the high he didn't know he was getting.

"Coach Broyles said, 'Jim, I didn't think you drank,'" Grizzle recalled. "I said, 'I don't drink.'"

It seems that Jim's hotel bill didn't reflect a teetotaler. While he was shelling out a little more for turtle soup, the players were souped out of their shells on his tab.

"They charged everything to me," Grizzle said of the drinks his teammates consumed, knowing he didn't drink. "I think it was $2,500, which was a whole lot of money back then. Royal Crown, [and] all that fancy stuff."

No doubt Jim doesn't drink if he thought Royal Crown was the fancy stuff.

Royal Crown Cola washes down a Moon Pie just fine, but Crown Royal presumably was the fancy stuff his teammates charged on his tab.

Grizzle probably deserved the unexpected bar bill, which, of course, he didn't have to pay.

COOKIE CON MAN

After all, he had conned cookies off some teammates, most notably Jerry Jones.

"Jerry Jones was the most gullible of the bunch," Grizzle said, "though he would get you back. You might come out to your car and find something had happened to your tires."

Probably fitting retribution for the crumb that conned him out of his cookies.

"I never heard Jerry's mother call him anything but honey," Grizzle recalled. "She made him a box of oatmeal cookies. It was so big I couldn't hardly carry them. Back then they thought chocolate was bad for your complexion. So I told Jerry, 'I want you to put your cookies in my room because I want to save your complexion.' And he said, 'Jimmy, you are so good to me.'

"But I'd see him eating one, and then maybe two or three. And I said, 'You start out with one and now you are up to two or three. Look what that's going to do to you.' In the meantime, we're eating on these cookies forever. And we get down to the bottom of them and there's a letter. And it says, 'Honey, so-and-so in North Little Rock had a bad car wreck.' And he comes running in there, and said, 'Jimmy, I didn't know you knew so-and-so.' I said, 'Hey, it's bad enough that you are getting into the cookies. I didn't say anything about reading my mail.'"

Grizzle allowed he did let Jones use his car.

"I had a car that used a quart of oil about every mile," Grizzle said. "Jerry didn't know that when he said, 'Jimmy, I need to go home. Can I borrow your car?' I said, 'Jerry it uses a little oil.' He says, 'That's all I right, I got some money to put more back in it.'

"He's about 20 miles from here and calls and says, 'I didn't know it used a quart a mile.' He blowed the motor up and put in a whole new motor. That was a heck of a deal for me. But I know he got me back some way. He was gullible, but he always got you back."

And always came to the front if you needed him.

"Jerry later took us to the Super Bowl," Grizzle said. "We were in the high-dollar suites, high-dollar everything and it didn't cost us a nickel."

WHO'S THE BOSS?

"Ronnie Caveness was tough, tough, tough," Grizzle said of the All-American linebacker. "But one year [Outland Trophy-winning defensive lineman] Loyd Phillips said, 'I'm going to be the boss.' Caveness and Loyd Phillips got in this room and it wasn't no wrasslin'. It was fighting to see who the boss was going to be. Finally, Caveness knocked Loyd's tooth out and Loyd said, 'I guess you are the boss.'"

And the two proceeded to lead the defense in stuffing offenses for the national championship team.

WEANING THE OPPOSITION

Wilson Matthews recalled grumping at another player because of Grizzle. "We're ahead of TCU," Matthews recalled, "but we're not ahead by much. And I see [defensive tackle] Tommy Brasher laughing. And I come up to him and say, 'What's so funny, Brasher? This game's not over!' And he says, 'I know, Coach, but that Grizzle...'

"'Oh,' I said, 'And just what did Grizzle say?'

"'Grizzle said,' Brasher relayed, 'Tommy, why don't you go over to the other side of the line and help those folks over there? I've done got 'em weaned from running to this side.'"

Quinn Grovey

Quinn Grovey

THANKS, REF

M ost players' memories of officials aren't good ones. Almost always, they remember what they deem a bad call and the official who made it.

But Quinn Grovey remains eternally grateful for the crew that officiated the Hogs' 38-20 win over Hawaii that closed the 1987 regular season in Honolulu.

Al Noga, Hawaii's massive nose guard, earned All-America honors, no doubt thanks in part to making several sack lunches a la Grovey.

"Al Noga was on me that whole game," Grovey said. "I remember one time he had me wrapped up and was just kind of walking, carrying me along. I wasn't going to let the guy show me up on national TV. I grabbed the football and boom! I hit him in the stomach. He slapped me in the head. I thought, 'Oh, oh, what have I done?' But the refs came and saved me."

DALLAS DISEASE

T hough they rank among the best ever statistically of Arkansas' quarterbacks, Quinn Grovey and Barry Lunney share a sickness about quarterbacking at Cotton Bowl Stadium in Dallas.

"Funny thing about being down there at the Cotton Bowl for the SMU game," Grovey said of 1998 when he was the sideline reporter on the Razorbacks' radio network while Lunney was then a Razorback graduate assistant coach. "I said, 'Man, the last time I came into this stadium [the

January 1, 1990 Cotton Bowl against Tennessee], I was as sick as a dog.' I caught flu before we played in the Cotton Bowl. And Barry Lunney comes around there and said, 'The last time I left this stadium I was as sick as a dog.'"

Though rallying the Hogs to get back in the game, Lunney fumbled on the goal line to end a 17-14 season opening loss to SMU in 1995, but then quarterbacked Danny Ford's Hogs to the 1995 SEC West championship.

Carlos Hall

MR. WRONG DOES IT RIGHT

D oing the wrong thing at the right time made Carlos Hall a Razorback hero–particularly to his coach, Houston Nutt.

Senior defensive end Hall was supposed to be pushing, not jumping, as he reared up to block the field goal, preserving Arkansas' 10-7 victory over South Carolina in 2001 at Little Rock.

"It's something we've worked on," Hall said, "but actually I wasn't supposed to do it. I just did it on my own. I was supposed to be in the line, too, trying to push through. But I said to myself, 'I've got to go get this. I am going to jump.' I got behind Jermaine Brooks and Curt Davis, those big boys, and they got a great push and I jumped behind them. I was supposed to line up at end, but I got behind them. I kinda did something out of the playbook. I knew it wasn't going through the upright because it hit my arm so hard. I just hit the ground saying, 'Yes!'"

So did the coaches. Better that Hall was at the wrong place to block the kick than at the right place to see the field goal made.

"It was a critical situation," defensive line coach Bobby Allen said. "We had him jumping in that situation early season but changed his role as teams read what he was doing. He went back to what was natural and thought, 'Hey, I'm going to get in there and jump.' Thank goodness he did. He overcame coaching, I'll be honest."

THE MEANING OF BEATING LOU

Houston Nutt can honestly say there is no coach over whom a victory means more than Lou Holtz.

Nutt was the sophomore Holtz inherited as the Razorback backup quarterback to Ron Calcagni in 1977 before Houston transferred to Oklahoma State the following year.

As a graduate assistant, Nutt rejoined Holtz and the Razorbacks in 1983 for Lou's Arkansas farewell.

"Anytime you beat Lou Holtz," Nutt said, "because of the relationship playing for him, and the mentorship, so many things he taught you–it's always big when you beat your teacher."

The 2001 game was the first real coaching clash between the two on a level field.

Arkansas had a healthy Clint Stoerner, and injury-plagued South Carolina was down to a fourth-string walk-on quarterback when the first Nutt-Holtz clash occurred, with Arkansas romping USC, 48-14, in 1999 at Little Rock.

In 2000, USC had the healthy quarterbacks and Arkansas the injured ones when Holtz's Gamecocks won, 27-7, in Columbia, S.C. Last year's victory before a vocal Little Rock crowd started Arkansas on a four-game SEC winning streak.

"The advantage was Little Rock, Arkansas," Nutt said. "The crowd, the atmosphere. It was very strong and came down to who made the fewest mistakes, except Carlos Hall doing the wrong thing at the right time."

Dan Hampton

Dan Hampton

JUST A COTTON PICKIN' MINUTE

Dan Hampton was just a Cotton Bowl away from throwing away an eventual All-American career with the Razorbacks that likely would have cost him his Hall of Fame career with the Chicago Bears.

The defensive tackle from Jacksonville, Arkansas, was ready to turn in his Razorback jersey as a freshman for Frank Broyles in 1975.

"About halfway through my freshman year," Hampton said, "I became disillusioned, and I wanted to leave–wanted to transfer to Univerisity of Central Arkansas. I didn't like the whole deal. We went to Dallas and the Cotton Bowl [and beat Georgia] and I said to myself, 'My God! This is the greatest thing in the world. You are playing major college football. What is wrong with you?' And I went back and kind of redoubled my efforts. I kind of said, 'I've got a great opportunity. Don't screw this up!' And that's really the way it worked. A lot of kids don't get it. I got it."

And the NFL scouts got to see it, which they may or may not have seen in the NAIA setting of UCA. Back then, UCA did not compare to the 10-2, 5-5-1, 11-1 and 9-2-1 Razorback teams that Hampton played for on the defensive line for Frank Broyles in 1975 and '76 and Lou Holtz in '77 and '78.

"Who knows if they would have found me or not if I had transferred?" Hampton said. "I was lucky."

THE GUNSMOKE INDIAN

S everal Sundays during Dan Hampton's All-American senior season of 1978, he hobbled into the training room so stove up and banged up from Saturday's game that even veteran Razorback trainers Dean Weber and former assistant Mike "Red" McDonald wondered how he possibly could play the following week. But he would, Hampton assured them.

"I'm just like one of those Indians on Gunsmoke," Hampton told them repeatedly. "You see Marshall Dillon shoot them down one week, and the next week there they are again. I kind of lived by that."

For a good 12 years, Hampton bounced back like the Gunsmoke Indian during a Hall of Fame career with the Chicago Bears.

"Even into the pros," Hampton said, "I carried that badge. Buddy Ryan [the Bears' former defensive coordinator] was a great influence on me as a pro. He said that you could play great one week and if the next two weeks you disappear–nobody wants that. You've got to play great all the time. So the only way to play great is to be there."

UNLIKELY ALL-AMERICANS

U CA almost got Jimmy Walker out of Little Rock Central before the 1975 season and Hampton out of Jacksonville once the season ended.

Instead it got neither, and Arkansas got a pair who became All-American defensive tackles as seniors in 1978.

"I can't ever remember Arkansas having two All-Americans at the same position in the same year," said Harold

Horton, who joined the UA as a player in 1957 and coached the 1978 defensive line.

"He didn't generate a lot of scholarship offers until after the high school all-star game," Hampton said of Walker. "And I wasn't a guy with a lot of college offers. We weren't guys a lot of colleges wanted, but we turned into pretty good players. Jimmy was happy to play for the Razorbacks and so was I.

"I remember the day that they told us we both made All-American. He was one of the good guys. A lot of times you have a running kind of a deal where you try and play off of each other, but Jimmy and I really got along, a great guy."

They were a contrast in styles. Hampton, a 6'5" weightlifter, was strong and rangy, and Walker was more of a squatty body, much like Melvin Bradley, who would star as a defensive lineman for Houston Nutt's Razorbacks in 1998 and '99.

"Jimmy was smaller and not a power player," Hampton said, "but he used his great quickness."

LIKE GRAMMAR SCHOOL

The coaches Hampton played for at Arkansas, both head coaches and assistants, read like a Who's Who.

Frank Broyles and Lou Holtz, both national championship winners, were his head coaches. Jimmy Johnson, who won a national championship and two Super Bowls as a head coach, Horton, who won two NAIA championships head coaching UCA, and Monte Kiffin, one of the most currently renowned defensive coordinators in the NFL, were assistants during his college career.

"They were wonderful," Hampton said. "They were great. They were like your teachers in grammar school and high school who had an impact on you that make a lasting impression, but you move on."

Lou Holtz's impression is the most vivid with Dan.

"Lou was really hands-on," Hampton said. "Everything that happened, you had to speak to the burning bush. He really was great. He had the do-right rule, and as long as you did things the right way, you had no problem. It was great playing for him. He treated you like men. And as long as you acted like it, everything was cool. Lou was the buck-stops-here kind of guy. That was cool. Because you knew where you stood at all times."

With bowl appearances during three of his four Arkansas years and the Bears becoming "Da Bears" with a Super Bowl title during Hampton's tenure, Dan was the man wherever he played ball.

"I was very fortunate," Hampton said. "I played in a great era of the Razorback where a lot of people cared about it back in the late '70s. And I played in a great era for the Bears from 1983-90. It takes a lot of people [doing] a lot of good things to generate that kind of interest. I was lucky to be a part of both those times. Man, it was really good!"

Steve Heim

A WELL-PLANNED UPSET

At least one Razorback thought big about annihilating mighty Oklahoma long before Lou Holtz's 1977 Razorbacks routed Barry Switzer's overwhelmingly favored Sooners, 31-6, at the Orange Bowl in Miami.

Of course, everything about Steve Heim was big. He was a 6'5" senior offensive tackle, ahead of his time, weighing 305 pounds back then.

Heim, now an orthopedist, was big, but the odds of Oklahoma routing Arkansas were bigger, according to the bookies at the time.

Both Barry Switzer's Sooners and Holtz's Hogs were 9-1 going into the bowl game and had lost narrowly to Texas. But the Sooners were deemed loaded and hungry, especially with top-ranked Texas getting upset by Notre Dame in the Cotton Bowl a few hours before Arkansas and Oklahoma met in the Miami moonlight.

OU had closed the regular season routing Nebraska, while Arkansas had needed a late touchdown pass to squeak by Texas Tech in the Hogs' season finale.

Then Arkansas lost All-American senior offensive right guard Leotis Harris to a knee injury scrimmaging in Fayetteville before the Miami trip. And finally, the capper, Holtz suspended his two top running backs, leading rusher Ben Cowins and fullback Micheal Forrest, and receiver Donny Bobo, for disciplinary reasons, and didn't take them to Miami.

"Oklahoma had four defensive All-Americans, which was unheard of," Heim recalled. "They had smashed Nebraska, 38-7, on Thanksgiving Day. Texas beating Oklahoma was a fluke. Notre Dame beats Texas. So it's, 'Oklahoma, just show up and you win the national championship.' But most people didn't have a clue how good Arkansas was. We had a month to prepare, but Oklahoma did exactly what they had done all year long. And Holtz changed up a myriad of things."

ONE FALSE STEP
AND IT'S LATER FOR SOONERS

Heim swears that upon seeing Holtz's game plan, he knew it was Oklahoma, not Arkansas, beset with big problems. He remained solidly convinced even with Cowins and Forrest suspended, with sophomore reserve Roland Sales replacing Cowins.

"I remember being in Larry Beightol's office," Heim said of his offensive line coach, "and Holtz was in there and they said, 'Heim, you can do this all night long.'"

"This" was the play out of the veer, most instrumental in springing Sales for an Orange Bowl record 205 yards rushing.

"One of the Tabor twins played in front of me for them at tackle," Heim said. "We knew exactly what he was going to do every play, what his responsibility was. He later played for the Giants. He lined up on the outside shoulder, and his responsibility was to contain. He was 250 or 260. I'd take a big, slow deliberate step with my left foot and he'd fly to the outside.

"And there was a linebacker who was 215 pounds. I don't care how fast he was and that he was an All-American, he didn't see me coming. It was a mismatch. I'd hit him right in the side. They had an All-American nose guard,

Reggie Kinlaw, and [center Rick] Shumaker and [left guard Chuck] Herman double-teamed him. We didn't block the tackle; he went unblocked. He'd jump out when we handed the ball off, and we had the double-team and my block. By the time he fell back inside it was too late. About the most he'd do is touch Roland's thigh pads as Roland went by.

"We had them outnumbered. That was the play we made all the yards on, over and over and over again. They never did make an adjustment. So we leave a tackle unblocked, and I weigh 100 pounds more than a guy I'm blindsiding. We changed a lot of plays, and Oklahoma did the same thing they did all year. It was suicide. They took us lightly, they really did. And they had dissension. A lot of those guys really didn't like each other. They were calling each other names during the game and stuff. And we had overachievers, like Larry Jackson; what a great linebacker to be so small. And Rick Shumaker, playing center at 230 soaking wet. And what a coaching staff, like a Who's Who."

1977 Razorback assistants Beightol, Monte Kiffin and Don Breaux are longtime NFL assistants. Beightol, Kiffin, Bob Cope, Harold Horton, Jesse Branch and Ken Turner off that staff later were collegiate head coaches.

FROM FRANK TO LOU

The previous three years, Heim had come out of Fort Smith Northside to play for Frank Broyles. He was a reserve on Broyles's last great team, the 1975 Cotton Bowl champions.

"Totally different," Heim said when asked to compare Broyles and Holtz. "Frank was an organizer. The old type–courtly, southern coach. He supervised everything from the tower or the stands. I remember Holtz's first practice, and

Holtz is right in the damn huddle with his glasses and all. That was unheard of. With Holtz I had a great year. That year was Cinderella. So I can't say anything bad about Holtz. He had his faults, but he did all right for me."

A GOOFY TWIST OF FATE

Heim has been ecstatic, and at first surprised, he admitted, with the success of old teammate Houston Nutt coaching the Hogs since 1998.

Nutt's only two years as a reserve Razorback quarterback coincided with Heim's junior and senior Razorback seasons.

"I remember when I thought he was just another goofus freshman," Heim recalled of Nutt breaking in with the '76 Hogs. "Obviously he has learned a lot. He brought enthusiasm, and that's the important thing.

"He's done well."

Orville Henry

WOODY WOULDN'T, WOULD HE?

Covering the Razorbacks for nearly 60 years, most of them while sports editor of the dearly missed *Arkansas Gazette*, helped make the late Orville Henry an Arkansas legend.

To fellow sportswriters attending the same press conferences, bowl banquets and such, Orville became as legendary at those events as he had so long been legendary at his typewriter.

Here are some examples: At one of those interminable Liberty Bowl luncheons, notorious for speakers patting on the back every Liberty Bowl worker who so much as picked up a candy wrapper, much less donated money to the bowl, former NCAA President Walter Byers was added to the speaking mix.

For some inexplicable reason, considering Arkansas and Georgia were the Liberty Bowl opponents, Byers began droning on and on about the late Woody Hayes, the Ohio State coaching curmudgeon.

"And Woody," Byers said expansively, "as you are looking down on us..."

"He's looking up," Orville interjected.

Byers looked startled as the room convulsed.

THE GOVERNOR'S THREE LITTLE WORDS

At the annual University of Arkansas Hall of Honor banquet, Arkansas Governor Mike Huckabee emceed.

The Governor had already bumbled once, lauding the just introduced Letterman's Club Alumni leader Mark Miller for being the man he saw quarterbacking Frank Broyles's 1975 Hogs to a Cotton Bowl victory over Georgia.

"I hate to bring this up," Miller said. "But I was moved to safety by then. Scott Bull was our quarterback at the Cotton Bowl."

Huckabee good-naturedly recovered from that gaffe and had picked up some steam until meandering into a too-long story about some prisoners of war clinging to three little words each time one was taken behind the prison to be tortured.

"These three little words kept them going," Huckabee kept saying, repeatedly building towards a climax and then backing off like a car lurching through a string of lights in a traffic jam. Finally, the good Governor supposed it was time to close. Pausing for emphasis, he said, "And do you know that those three little words were?"

"Woo, Pig, Sooie," Orville interrupted.

Uproarious laughter drowned out Huckabee's reply, "Return with Honor," the theme of the governor's Hall of Honor address.

SOURED CITRUS

At the Citrus Bowl press conference a couple of days before Houston Nutt's 1998 Hogs played Michigan in Orlando, Michigan Coach Lloyd Carr was being the typical Big Ten stoneface.

Then came a miracle. Some questions about the then new bowl championship series triggered Carr's interest.

Suddenly he began talking up a storm and avidly took follow-up questions about the BCS.

This soured the citrus of the Orlando corporate yuppie presiding over the press conference.

"Please, please," the moderator admonished. "We want you to restrict your questions just about our bowl game."

"Okay," Orville responded. "I've got a question about your bowl game. Is Orlando always this cold and rainy?"

BCS questions seemed mighty appropriate to the deflated Orlando booster after that.

ORVILLE'S MEMORIAL SERVICE

At Orville's memorial service the Saturday after his death in March of 2002, longtime *Arkansas Gazette* and *Arkansas Democrat-Gazette* sportswriter Jim Bailey remarked, "One of his favorite sayings was, 'Guessing is sometimes necessary. But there's nothing like knowing.' He always managed put himself in position to know."

Bailey also related how Orville broke in a new UA sports information director to the importance of the *Arkansas Gazette* in 1974.

Bill Curl was one of the nicest guys ever to work at the UA, but hired from Tulane, he wasn't prepared for Orville. On the eve of Arkansas opening the season against powerful Southern California in War Memorial Stadium, Orville wanted a sixth press pass for a story angle he had just thought about.

"He asked for a sixth press pass," Bailey related, "and was told, 'Sorry, Orville. The press box is booked to overflowing. We've had to turn down requests. You already have five passes.' Orville listened until he heard, 'I'm sorry, but we have to give fair and balanced treatment to all the media.'

"Orville said, 'Oh, does that mean we are supposed to treat you like State Teachers College?' He got the extra pass."

NICKED ON A NICKNAME

Also speaking at Orville's service, longtime *Gazette* political columnist and editorial writer Ernie Dumas said, "A lot of people have the notion that the sports pages are the less serious side of the paper–that they encourage frivolous writing. But to Orville they were serious."

As a young news writer, Dumas recalled being occasionally pressed into sports service for time and a half. He and the others would take dictation for the avalanche of Friday night high school football games called in from every county.

"There was a fullback from Prescott named Stanley," Dumas said, "who scored six touchdowns. And we wrote, 'Stanley the Steamer scored six touchdowns to lead the Prescott Curley Wolves...' The next day I received a memo."

> *Dumas,*
> *If in the Gazette's A-Section, you decide to write Governor Winthrop (I Just Had One Drink) Rockefeller, that's up to you. But in the sports pages, leave the nicknames to those who know what they are writing about.*

ABSENT THOUGHTS OF THE ABSENT-MINDED

Working closely for Orville for 14 years at the *Arkansas Gazette* often had this writer traveling the same mental wavelength as his boss.

Mostly that made for a good combination, but not always, as our wives will attest.

Once, when my wife, Nancy, and I returned from a long bowl trip, we found some unexpected flowers given to us by Herman Tuck, the longtime proprietor of Herman's Ribhouse in Fayetteville, and his wife, Irene. The flowers, we were later told, were for a feature that Nancy had done for an area newspaper on Herman's late father as part of a series on those who had cast a positive influence on Fayetteville during the 1950s.

However, having just returned tired from a long absence, we just couldn't initially fathom why Herman Tuck would send flowers.

"Maybe Herman is sick," I mused absent-mindedly.

Nancy's jaw dropped to the floor. Only an idiot, she reminded me, would suggest that someone sick would, out of the blue, send get-well flowers to someone healthy.

Feeling compelled to tell someone she had married a moron, Nancy called Orville's wife, Ann, and relayed the tale. Much chuckling ensued before they finally hung up.

Ten minutes later, Ann called, laughing even more than before.

She had relayed the tale to Orville, right through the "Maybe Herman is sick" part.

Apparently Orville didn't laugh.

"Herman's not sick," Orville responded, "but Irene hasn't been well."

Sometimes great minds think alike, our wives surmised, but concluded that in their husbands' case, like minds don't think at all.

That was okay with me. Even if the category was being absent-minded, somehow getting lumped with Orville meant you had been lumped with the best.

Lou Holtz

Lou Holtz

LOU'S FLY PATTERN

Much of former Arkansas coach Lou Holtz's humor was fairly contrived, but he did get off a few pretty good zingers during his 1977-83 Razorback tenure.

Once when discussing upcoming opponent Rice to a postpractice gathering of reporters, Holtz said, "The Rice Owls have a wide-open offense, but not as wide open as [this] young man's fly right here."

Six reporters glanced nervously down and then glanced up with relief.

The seventh turned more crimson than Alabama's Crimson Tide.

LOU'S LOST LUGGAGE

A local airline called Skyways, "Scareways" to the locals, operated out of Fayetteville during Lou's Razorback era.

"I called up Skyways," Holtz related. "And I asked them if I brought out three pieces of luggage, could they send one to New York, one to Chicago and one to Los Angeles. They said, 'No, sir. We can't do that.' And I said, 'That's funny, you did it the last time when I was flying to Memphis.'"

On another occasion, Lou quipped of Skyways, "They don't sell tickets. They sell chances."

RICE KRISPIED

A shocking 17-16 loss to lowly Rice under the lights in Little Rock in 1980 may have been Lou Holtz's most galling defeat during his Arkansas tenure.

Taping his TV show right after the game at War Memorial Stadium, Lou eschewed the standard opening introduction from announcer/cohost Paul Eells and opened the show himself.

"Welcome to the *Lou Holtz Show*," said Lou. "Unfortunately, I'm Lou Holtz."

FASTEST TO OBLIVION

Holtz once damned with faint praise a fast but scatterbrained defensive back.

"He has 4.3 speed," Holtz said, "which means he gets to the wrong place faster than anybody else."

NO MO PROBLEMS

For a brief period, Lou Holtz had a lineman named Mo on the Razorback roster.

Not brief enough for Lou, who always seemed at odds with the lineman. The situation resolved quickly.

"I've looked at your grades," Holtz was reported to have said. "Soon there'll be no mo' Mo."

STAGE FRIGHT

Bruce Lahay became one of Arkansas' best ever pooch-punters and developed into an All-American placekicker as a fifth-year senior.

As a freshman, though, the St. Louis-born kicker got stage fright every time head coach Lou Holtz saw him kick.

"I just can't kick with him around," Lahay nervously confessed to kicking coach Ken Turner.

"Better get used to it," Turner wryly advised. "I've got a hunch he's going to be at all the games."

COMPARING BURNT ORANGES

Former Razorback NCAA outdoor 1,500-meter champion Frank O'Mara once halfheartedly denied this happened, but it nonetheless became an oft-told part of Razorback folklore. Knowing the Irishman's irreverent dry wit, one can imagine that it did occur.

O'Mara, running for a Razorback cross-country team that was, by then, nine years into a Southwest Conference championship streak, and his mates were cutting up inside the Broyles Complex after a workout. This annoyed Lou Holtz as he put the football team through its practice paces preparing for Texas.

"Hey! Hey!" Holtz shouted at the talkative tracksters. "Don't you know this is Texas week?!"

"What's the blooming fuss about?" O'Mara reportedly replied. "Texas never gives us any trouble."

WHO WOULD KNOW
BETTER, INDEED

Early during the week interim between the end of the 1983 season and the Sunday that he was fired, Lou Holtz started purging his staff.

Lou canned a few and then took to the recruiting trail, belatedly trying to recover from the area he ignored that proved his Arkansas undoing.

Since Lou wasn't around for comment, some of the coaches informed media they indeed had been fired.

Finally, reached for comment, Holtz wouldn't definitely say he had fired some assistants.

Told that the coaches had said they had been fired, Lou replied, with this mysterious nonanswer: "Who would know better than they?"

Later in the week, the issue about whether Holtz had done radio commercials endorsing North Carolina Senator Jesse Helms became a hot item.

This got into politics, which put it in the news domain of the newspapers as much as sports.

When an *Arkansas Gazette* state desk reporter asked Holtz about the commercials, Lou said, "You need to be asking the Jesse Helms people about that."

"Well, Coach," the reporter responded, "who would know better than you?"

Dead silence...then Holtz did offer his own explanation.

Harold Horton

PILING ON HAROLD

L iterally from the bottom of the pile, DeWitt's Harold Horton rose to Razorback Hall of Honor prominence.

Harold was a starter for Frank Broyles's first three Southwest Conference championship teams from 1959-61, a Razorback linebacker coach for Broyles from 1968-76, a Razorback defensive line coach for Lou Holtz from 1977-80, a two-time NAIA championship coach at the University of Central Arkansas, and since 1990, variously the Razorbacks' recruiting coordinator, director of football operations and current vice president of the Razorback Foundation.

Back in 1958, though, after being a freshman in 1957 under Jack Mitchell, Horton was a sophomore redshirting scout-team scrub buried in the morass of Broyles's 0-6 Razorback start.

The only folks hotter than Broyles about the 0-6 start were hot-tempered defensive coordinator Jim MacKenzie and hotter-tempered linebacker coach Wilson Matthews, a legend for his intensity and success.

"They worked the dog out of us," Horton recalled. "I can remember in that 0-6 start Coach Matthews keeping the scout team after practice a lot of times. He'd just run us and run us and run us. But there were so many of us that he couldn't run us off."

Harold couldn't possibly run when MacKenzie and Matthews piled it on.

"I remember against Rice when we lost in '58, we had done a poor job rushing the passer," Horton recalled. "The next week on the scout team, George McKinney, Darrell Williams, myself and Kerry Ahrens alternated being the quarterback, dropping back until every player got on the pile. Not just the front seven, the total 11. I don't know if they were trying to make them tough, but us people who had to absorb that, we took a beating.

"MacKenzie and Matthews were the two instigators. I remember at the time Coach Broyles blaming the scout team because we were getting beat. Blaming the scout team! We'd look at ourselves. They'd run us to the point so late in practice that when we went to the cafeteria to eat the cafeteria would be closed. Finally the captains went to the coaching staff and got that stuff changed. It was tough."

LOU'S APOLOGY

Horton had all sorts of big moments as a Razorback coach, including coaching in the 1969 Shootout and coaching defensive MVPs Cliff Powell in the 1970 Sugar Bowl, Hal McAfee in the 1976 Cotton Bowl, and Reggie Freeman in the 1978 Orange Bowl.

What makes him a rare breed on our planet is that he received an apology from Lou Holtz.

Holtz fired Horton and defensive coordinator Bob Cope after the 1980 season to make way for new coordinator Don Lindsey and Lindsey's staff.

"Ten years later I get a message to call Lou," Horton said. "I was here as recruiting coordinator and had come back from a high school coaching clinic. There was a note from Lou Holtz to call. I called twice and couldn't reach him. Then Lou called. He said 'I've got two things to tell you. Number one: I met a very well groomed young man who was very polite and stuck out his hand and said, 'I'm Tim Horton.'"

Tim is Harold's son and a former Razorback receiver of renown for Ken Hatfield from 1986-89. He is currently an assistant at the Air Force Academy.

"'Any way I can help him in the coaching profession,' Holtz said, 'let me know. The second thing: I fired a lot of coaches in my coaching career. Most I fired, they deserved it. But when I fired you, I was wrong. I made a mistake. I listened to one person, and I was wrong to listen to that one person.'

"I said, 'Coach, you don't have to apologize to me. Because what you did opened another door. You got me out of a rut and gave me the opportunity to be a head coach, and I had eight of the greatest years I could ask for.'"

AT LEAST NOT SLUGGED

Lou had the temper, but apparently nobody was more uptight than Charlie Coffey, the defensive coordinator for Broyles in 1969 when Harold, often called "Squirrel," was a second-year linebacker coach getting ready for the Big Shootout with Texas.

"I remember in '69," Horton said. "the defensive staff is in the half-house looking out the window and Texas runs on the field. I turn to Charlie Coffey and I said, 'Dang, Charlie! Look how big they are!' Charlie popped me on the chest and said, '%@# Squirrel! Shut up.'"

He was so tense. That 1969 staff still gets together every year. There's a bond there. We were all close. And that was true on Lou's staffs when [former defensive coordinator] Monte Kiffin was here."

WINGING IT AWAY FROM HOME

Harold and Tim are about as close as a father and son can be, but Tim knows he's needed distance from Arkansas to develop as a coach in his own right.

Considering the ups and downs Tim has seen in coaching since the night he made fun of the fat kicker, it's a wonder he coaches at all.

"My mom and dad," Tim said from his Air Force office in Colorado Springs, "are everything I want to be in terms of parents and the work ethic they both have. But I'll always be Coach Horton's son. That's certainly not a bad thing, but I wanted to sprout my own wings. And in North Carolina and out here I'm Tim Horton, not Harold Horton's son."

Mike Ihrie

MIKE IHRIE: EXPOSING THE NAKED TRUTH

Mike Ihrie wouldn't publicly unveil the naked truth about another football player's identity other than that he was a "big old lineman," but years later, Mike exposed the exotic show performed in front of a window of the Wilson Sharp Athletic Dorm.

Ihrie was a Razorback offensive lineman from 1980-83 for Lou Holtz and inherited as a fifth-year by Ken Hatfield in 1984.

The show, performed during the Holtz era, was unbeknownst to the coach until after its opening night. It was an unexpected, and no doubt undesired, eyeful for basketball fans walking past Wilson Sharp on the way to Barnhill Arena to see Eddie Sutton's Hogs.

"Remember the *Gong Show* with the Unknown Comic?" Ihrie asked. "Well, we had the Unknown Dancer, with a grocery bag over his head, dancing nude in the window with the lights flashing on and off. Meanwhile [reserve quarterback-cornerback] Randy Wessinger would be out on Stadium Drive telling the crowd, 'Come one, come all! See the nude exotic dancer of Wilson Sharp!' The next day, Eddie Sutton came up raising hell, and Lou Holtz calls a team meeting and says, 'Hey! Hey! There will be no more nude dancing any more before basketball games!'"

CAUCASIAN PERSUASION

For all his harshness, Lou did have a sensitive side. When one of the black players married a white woman, Holtz took pains to tell all the players that race wasn't important, but love was.

"He said," Ihrie recalled, 'There is no reason why marital relationships between blacks and Caucasians can't be successful.'

Holtz then felt a gentle nudge.

'Coach,' a player corrected, 'she's not Caucasian. She's German.'"

THE PRICE OF FAME

Just about every college with a football team has legends about players whose football prowess got them out of all sorts of jams.

Mike Ihrie wasn't one of them.

"I got pulled over for speeding through Mountainburg," Ihrie recalled. "The cop says, 'Hello, Mario.'

"I said, 'I'm not Mario. I'm Mike Ihrie; I play football for the Razorbacks.'

"'Oh,' the cop replied. 'The way you are driving, I thought you were Mario Andretti.'"

All "Mario" got to autograph was a ticket.

Ihrie had another driving incident, well, actually a passenger incident, where he paid the penalty for a teammate's prowess.

"We were about to go to Baylor for the game in '82," Ihrie said. "I'm riding to the airport with [starting quarterback] Brad Taylor and [reserve quarterback] Scott Reid. Brad gets into an argument with somebody before we go and it goes on for 20 minutes before I pull him away. We are supposed to be at the airport, and the plane is on the runway with the engines going."

In walks Ihrie, Taylor, and Reid. "Lou says, 'I can't believe you, Mike Ihrie, holding up your teammates. [Offensive line coach] Larry Beightol says, 'Yeah, Ihrie, you piece of crap.' Later I'm by myself and Lou comes up still chewing me out. I said, 'Coach, who do you think I rode with?' Lou said, 'Oh, well, I'm not mad at you. Let's just keep this between us.'"

Holtz could have leveled Reid, too, since he apparently didn't want to rattle his sophomore quarterback Taylor before his first start of '82.

However, he had to keep Reid intact, because Scott was too valuable as Taylor's interpreter.

Taylor, you see, was the kind of quarterback who drove Lou crazy.

Lou wanted them programmed like Tom Jones, the senior starter for most of '82, and Kevin Scanlon before him, who knew what everyone did on every play and what Holtz expected to the last detail.

Taylor played sandlot style, using his great arm and great instincts without any cause to examine the why of what got achieved.

Reid, though without Jones's or Scanlon's ability, was also that blackboard Holtz style of quarterback, as manifested by his now being a successful high school coach.

"Lou would be in a team meeting," Ihrie said, "and say something like, 'Brad Taylor, on this 43XYZ when the corner squats and a linebacker blitzes and so-so stunts, who do you throw to?'

"And Brad would scratch his head and say, 'The guy that's open?'

"Lou would get so mad. Then he'd go Scott Reid. 'On play 43XYZ who do you throw to?' And Scott would answer something like, 'The tight end on the dump route, because the corner will react to the receiver's out and up while the linebacker blitzes...'

"And Lou would smile, 'That's right.'

"So then Lou would ask Brad again, and you could hear Scott whispering, and Brad would answer what Scott told him. And Lou would say, 'Good meeting.'"

SLEEPING IN

Lou's arduous football routine made for sleepy players, none too fired up about leaping out of bed to go to class.

Lou took care of that. He instituted mandatory attendance for breakfast with a postpractice bed check requiring players NOT to be back in their rooms asleep after breakfast.

So if they didn't have class, you'd see forlorn players hanging around the Student Union.

Except you'd never see offensive guard Darryl Pickett.

"Darryl beat the bed check," Ihrie recalled. "At each room in Wilson Sharp, they had a vanity closet with shelves. He took the shelves out, signed in for breakfast and then would go back to his room and sleep in the shelves like Dracula."

Joe Kines

Joe Kines

IN THE INTERIM

Defensive coordinator Joe Kines became Arkansas' interim head coach in 1992 when athletic director Frank Broyles fired Jack Crowe after a 10-3 season opening loss to The Citadel.

Of his title, Kines remarked, "Aren't we all interim?"

GASP!

After being named head coach, Kines's first postpractice press conference sounded like an obscene phone call.

He was still serving as defensive coordinator, but felt the need to know what was happening with the struggling offense that only mustered a field goal against The Citadel.

So Kines raced around both ends of the field, exhorting and encouraging.

Thus, the tape of every postpractice press conference began with the coach's heavy breathing.

Greg Koch

FROM GRIDIRON TO COURTROOM

G reg Koch traces his metamorphosis from football to lawyering to a lack of equipment.

"That one year I didn't wear a helmet," Koch said, "I decided to become a lawyer."

No one at Arkansas from 1973-76 doubted that Koch, a former Razorback and standout NFL offensive lineman, had the mind to be in law.

They just wondered which side of the law.

Koch and running buddy R. C. Thielemann, friends since their Spring Woods High School days in Houston, were always on the edge of Coach Frank Broyles's doghouse, but they were also in the starting line since the third game of 1973.

Thielemann also went on to a long NFL career.

"I think we'll be linked together for the rest of our lives," Koch said. "When somebody sees R. C., it's 'Where's Greg?' And when somebody sees me they are expecting to see R. C. We were best friends in high school and best friends here. We were a little different back then. We've all grown up now and have kids and families. But we had a great time. R. C. is a mortgage broker now living in Atlanta."

DON'T THROW ME INTO THAT BRIAR PATCH

T he most publicized trouble that Koch and Thielemann got into made them the envy of the team.

"I guess the biggest deal we ever did was when Frank [Broyles] kicked us out of the athletic dorm," Koch said. "It was the spring of '74. We got into an altercation with about five fraternities. It was just R. C. and me and there were about 40 fraternity guys. It should have been a mismatch, except R. C. had the habit of carrying a machete in his car. I don't know why he had it, but when I pulled that machete out there were about 40 fraternity guys who were running for their fraternities. Later that night, R. C. and I were spending the night in the Fayetteville jail. So Frank said, 'You guys will not be spending the next football season in the dorm.' It did give us a little wake-up call."

Their social scene was a whole lot better than when they were housed in the all-male Wilson Sharp Athletic Dormitory.

"If Frank were to know..." Koch said. "It was a beautiful thing, because he kicked us down to Pomfret, which was a coed dorm, and still allowed us to eat at the training table. So we still had the good food but didn't have any curfew and were living in a dorm with girls that we liked. We started thinking about what we could do to get kicked down to Pomfret the next year, but it didn't work out like that."

Richard LaFargue

Richard LaFargue

WHIRLPOOL TREATMENTS

Those who didn't believe Richard LaFargue's or-neriness were all wet—sometimes literally, if they were too close to the training room whirlpool.

"Let me tell you," LaFargue said, "the day after we beat Baylor, 41-3, and got 600 yards offense, [offensive coordinator] Bo Rein comes in the training room with all the offensive stats, and all his clothes from church on, Sunday shoes and all. So Gerald Skinner and I come up on either side of him and walk him to the edge of the whirlpool like we're going to dunk him. Next thing I know, Skinner goes boink, and Bo Rein goes whoosh. All the stats, all his clothes, billfold, everything is sopped. He goes to the locker room, changes into sweats and says, 'If you sons of bitches didn't have 600 yards offense yesterday, you would be running from now until tomorrow morning.' He was so mad, but he says, 'You all played so good I can't run you.'"

A few years later, as the head coach at LSU, Rein died in a recruiting trip plane crash.

Angry as Rein was after being dumped in the UA whirlpool, he was angrier the night before in Waco, Texas—though not as angry as Broyles.

Usually big Bible-study buddies with then Baylor coach Grant Teaff, Broyles preached Old Testament an-eye-for-an-eye the night Ronnie Lee, Baylor's 270-pound tight end, waylaid Arkansas kicker Steve Little as Little still was on his game-opening kickoff follow through.

It knocked Little out of the game.

"Frank comes off the field so mad," LaFargue said. "He says, 'Hurt them. Let's put it on them. Let's hurt 'em.'"

"We proceed to unleash 41 points on them, and they had to carry that guy off the field."

Of course Baylor claimed Lee wasted Little without malice aforethought.

"R. C. and Greg knew their linebacker from high school in Houston," LaFargue said. "During the game, the Baylor coaches said it had been a fluke deal. But the guy Greg and R. C. knew told them it was a set-up deal. They had practiced it all week. The guy was five yards off sides! They took a weapon out of the game, but it backfired on them. We were so fired up. We were running quarterback sneaks from the nine-yard line and scoring. Marvin Daily [a fifth-year senior tight end] kicked extra points, and he hadn't kicked since he was in high school at Alma."

Jim Lindsey

LEARNING THE FOUR DON'TS

They don't rank with the Ten Commandments, but Frank Broyles's "Four Don'ts of the Kicking Game" are a code to live by, Jim Lindsey, former wingback, said. They form, he said, the biggest lesson he learned at the UA.

"The four dont's of the kicking game," Lindsey said. "Don't rough the kicker. Don't be off side. Don't let the ball hit the ground. And don't clip.

"Don't rough the kicker; it's wrong to hit a man when he's defenseless. Don't be off side. It's wrong to unfairly get the jump on somebody when it's against the rules. Don't let the ball hit the ground is the same as don't squander opportunity. Take advantage of it. Don't be stupid and let things roll against you. And clipping...you do everything right and some fool clips. Because normally, a clip doesn't have anything to do with a play. So two things you shouldn't do to others and the other two are things you shouldn't do to yourself."

GROUND HOG'S DAY

Lindsey may have revered the late Bill Ferrell, the trainer/baseball coach called "Ground Hog" or "Groundy," more than any of the Razorback icons he still remembers as legends.

"I remember," Lindsey said, "the day we played Texas. The night before, we had seen the movie *Fail Safe*. And Jerry Jones is in the training room getting taped, and so am

I. And he says, 'What do you think of that movie? And I said, 'It was unbelievable.'

"And he said, 'Do you think any of that could ever happen?'

"And I said, 'I don't know. What do you think?'

"And he said, 'Groundy, what do you think?'

"And Groundy said, 'I don't know a damned thing about that movie. But I know some boys who are about to get their ass whipped by Texas.'"

Groundy motivated as a trainer but learned motivation from the master, Bowden Wyatt, the coach who inherited a struggling program and browbeat it into being a Southwest Conference champion two years later in 1954.

"He had some great stories about Bowden Wyatt," Lindsey said. "He said Bowden Wyatt would make all the coaches leave before he'd give the pregame pep talk. They were playing Ole Miss, the one they won with the pass to Preston Carpenter, in Little Rock. They had already warmed up and had gone back in and were fixing to come back out and play. Bowden says, 'Men, all of us have looked at the film this week. You know they are better than us. They outweigh us 26 pounds per man. They are bigger than us. I watched them warming up. They are faster than us. They are faster, they are bigger, they are better. But somehow, some way we are going to beat those sons of bitches!' Groundy said it was chilling the way he could handle a team."

While Bowden Wyatt reportedly motivated with an intimidating glare, Wilson Matthews could motivate with a roar, and Frank Broyles could motivate like an evangelical preacher, Bill Ferrell motivated like a fatherly Southerner from old Virginia, which he most certainly was.

"Bill Ferrell was so courtly," Lindsey said, "and he knew how to reach kids. Groundy and Dr. [Coy] Kaylor [the lone orthopedist for Northwest Arkansas and Fort Smith in the

1950s and '60s] were just wonderful. When we beat Texas Tech [in 1965] and went to the Cotton Bowl and played LSU, we gave Dr. Kaylor and Groundy game balls. Nobody knows how much success was attributed to them."

Years of ministering to athletes apparently made Bill Ferrell more of a psychologist than some who endeavor to practice it today.

"We had a boy who was a bad person," Lindsey recalled of his Razorback days. "And Groundy said, 'Well, he's had a lot of tough circumstances. He's an orphan and what he's endured would have been a hard time for all of us. But, with all that, he's rotten. And he will mess up a whole barrel of apples.' He was a genius."

Lindsey recalled how Ferrell made a good apple a great one.

Tommy Burnett, the middle of the three great Burnett brothers who excelled as running backs, was a promising back always dinged by little injuries.

Burnett's infrequent availability had him on second team starting the August preseason, though he had been deemed first-team material at the end of spring practice.

"Tommy was really upset and complaining about it," Lindsey recalled. "He kept saying it was wrong. Groundy heard it and talked to Tommy. Groundy said, 'You are like a spring flower, son. You wilt in the fall. You haven't proven to them you are better than that. And you haven't proven that to me.' Well, that year Tommy went out and played great and he never complained."

AN UNBEARABLE TALE

For those that couldn't comprehend Bill Ferrell's old Southern style motivation, there was always Wilson Matthews.

Wilson could motivate with veins bulging in his neck yet make you laugh at the same time. Bear with me.

"I remember we are playing Baylor at Waco," Lindsey said of visiting the Bears, "and Wilson says, 'You know they've got that damned bear out there in that cage. I hate that son of a bitch. They let him walk around the sideline with two people holding him on the cords. If any of you are knocked out of bounds on the sidelines and are close to that son of a bitch, you have my full authority to kick him in the nuts.'"

Scott Long

Scott Long

GLUE TO THE TEAM

S cott Long recalled rooming with Owen Kelly at the Ramada in Conway the night before a Little Rock game in 1991.

"Owen's earpiece for his Walkman broke," Long said, "and he walked to the convenience store next door and bought some Super Glue. Our room was so nice we decided to preserve its beauty exactly as it was. We Super Glued the room. The ice bucket, the coffeemaker, the remote control. Everything. We still felt unfulfilled, so we glued the chairs to the table. We left Saturday morning and did not think a thing about it until Dean Weber [the trainer also in charge of travel] got a call from the hotel."

Bill Johnson, in the first of his two one-year stints, nine years apart, coaching Razorback defensive linemen, was summoned to mete out the discipline. "He began to yell as he guided us outside for our actions," Long said. "The madder he tried to get, the more he began to laugh at us. He would turn around and try to get mad again, but then just laugh again. But he ran us anyway."

NEEDING A SHOT

T he late Shannon Wright had a troubled life but a quick wit.

Long recalled the Hogs' linebacker interjecting that wit in 1990 during a game against Houston, one of the many teams that the 3-8 Arkansas team couldn't slow down, much less stop.

Joe Pate was Jack Crowe's defensive coordinator in '90.

"Before the game," Long said, "Coach Pate had planned on a lot of blitzing. Coach Pate said we were going to 'load the gun and fire all the bullets.' Houston kept driving. Shannon kept looking to the sideline for the signal, and Coach Pate kept calling base defense and base coverage. Shannon started jumping up and down in front of the huddle, signaling with his hands and screaming toward the sideline. Jack Crowe called a timeout and summoned Shannon. He asked Shannon what was wrong. Shannon was exasperated and quickly blurted out: 'It's time to fire the damn bullets. They are killing us out there!'"

BATHROOM HUMOR

With penance paid for their Super Glue stunt, Long and Kelly were road roommates again in '91 when Crowe's Hogs played TCU in Fort Worth.

Long said that Kelly, of Wichita Falls, Texas, used the restroom upon checking into the hotel and then started phoning his Texas relatives. Long, later about to use the restroom, noticed that the toilet had malfunctioned and was flooding. "I said," Long recalled, "'Owen, the toilet's broken.' He ignored me and went on calling relatives. I waited a few minutes and then said again, 'Owen, the toilet is broken.' Irritated, he said, 'All right,' and just kept on talking. I wait another five minutes and say again, 'Owen, the toilet's broken.' This time very agitated, Owen responded, 'ALL RIGHT!'

"Then he glanced over to see [that] the water had flowed out of the bathroom and was soaking half the room. He slammed the phone down, grabbed some shoes and splashed into the bathroom. Once the water stopped, an angry Owen asked me why I hadn't done anything. I reminded him I told him three times but he did not listen. I made fun of him for splashing in there, and then he pointed out the joke was on me. He had pulled on my shoes."

GOD BLESS US, EVERY ONE

John Brooks never was much of a player during his tenure as a Razorback offensive lineman for Ken Hatfield and then Jack Crowe, but he graduated from the UA with honors and was one of the smartest players on the team. Except once.

Asked by Crowe to say a blessing at the Razorbacks' pregame meal in Conway before a Little Rock game, Brooks, according to Long, said, "Dear Lord, please bless this food...and...um...Lord...bless...um...please, Lord...bless us, God...um...Lord...please...um..."

"Immediately," Long said, "John was given the nickname 'Reverend.'"

HOLD ALL MY CALLS

Long recalled the constantly ringing phone of Razorback freshman defensive lineman Steven Berry in his Wilson Sharp Dormitory room.

"His phone rang off the hook," Long said. "It rang and rang and rang. Finally, someone asked him why he never answered it. His only reply was he 'did not know who was calling.' We tried to explain that was a reason to answer it, but it never hit home. He transferred after one semester."

Patrick Martin

Patrick Martin

THY STAFF THREW A ROD

Patrick Martin may be the only Razorback ever tripped by his own staff.

After a stunning touchdown pass from Ron Calcagni to Robert Farrell in the waning minutes put Lou Holtz's 1977 Hogs ahead of Texas A&M, 26-20, at the Aggies' Kyle Field in College Station, cornerback Martin thwarted a furious Aggie.

Martin intercepted a pass and then was brought down by a sideline Benedict Arnold.

"Monte Kiffin tackled me," Martin said of the defensive coordinator for Holtz's Hogs from 1977-79. "I intercepted it in the end zone and I thought I could score. I was pretty sure it would be a record. Here he comes out at midfield and I'm going, 'Coach! Coach! Time is still running!' Before I know it, he's tackling me, and my teammates are all over me, too, and the game is over. It's something that's strong in my mind even today. We were so happy to win. It was a blessing."

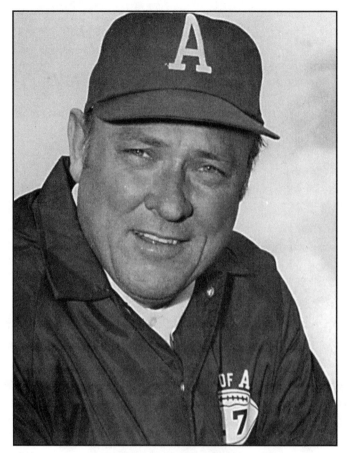

Wilson Matthews

Wilson Matthews

ARKANSAS' LIVING LEGEND

Anybody with a sense of Razorback history knows Wilson Matthews was a living legend. Until the night he died in 2002, Arkansas' associate athletic director emeritus was still as fiery and vibrant at 80 as he was when he ran the Razorback Foundation, coached Frank Broyles's linebackers, and before all that, set high school coaching records at Little Rock Central likely never to be duplicated.

Arkansas associate athletic director Bill Gray once said there are three true pioneers of the Razorbacks: athletic director Frank Broyles, sportswriter Orville Henry, who since has passed on, and Wilson Matthews, who died the same year Orville did.

Doing Wilson Matthews justice would fill this book, so I'll try and do the next best thing and recall Wilson's own favorite stories.

FINALLY A HIT

It only took one story that longtime sportswriter Jim Bailey loves to tell about Matthews to get Wilson started on some anecdotes a couple of years ago.

According to Bailey, during the 0-5 start to Broyles's first season coaching the Razorbacks, a fight broke out in practice.

"Wilson!" Broyles shouted from his tower according to Jim. "Wilson, break that up!"

"What for, Coach?" Matthews replied. "That's the first good lick I've seen all year."

Wilson shook his head on the retelling.

"I don't remember that," Matthews said.

Then he smiled.

"'Course, it could have happened," Matthews said. "It probably did."

The next tales all come from Wilson himself.

GRIZZLY TALE

Wayne Harris was his best player, and Jim Grizzle, a longtime tire magnate in Fort Smith and a Razorback defensive end for the 1964 national championship team, was his funniest player, Matthews said.

Wilson spun some "Grizzly" tales.

"We were on a bus after going to the picture show the night before we played TCU," Matthews said. "[Defensive coordinator] Jim MacKenzie and I are in the front seat and Grizzle and [eventual Dallas Cowboys owner] Jerry Jones are in the seat behind them. And I hear Jerry say, 'Grizzle, I'm going to be a millionaire before I'm 35. What do you think about that?'

"Grizzle said, 'Well, Jones, you may be. But I can buy and sell your ass by the time I'm 35.'

"Jones said, 'How you going to do that, Grizz?' And he said, 'Recapping tires.'

"And there's no telling how much money Grizzle's got. Of course one time I asked him if he was making as much as Jerry Jones. And he said, 'Aw, that pissant.'"

Matthews had another Grizzle tale.

"He started officiating high school ball, and he was the umpire for one particular ballgame," Matthews said. "The quarterback threw a pass, and Grizzle jumped up and caught it. The story goes when he caught it he turned around and pitched it to an end. Somebody asked him, 'Grizzle, why in the hell did you catch that pass?' And Grizz said, 'Well, hell, he hadn't caught one all night. I thought I'd catch one for him.'

"Grizzle was a character. You'd call a lightning stunt where he was supposed to come from the outside, and hell, he'd be out in the flat intercepting a pass. Or he'd be supposed to be out in the flat and he'd be rushing the passer making the tackle. Finally, I figured it didn't make any difference what in the hell you'd call. He was going to do whatever the hell he pleased. But he could play."

BILLY MOORE AND FIDEL

What about Billy Moore, the quarterback-defensive back of 1960-62 and alleged hellraiser whose older brother Henry, starred for Wilson at Central and also starred for the Razorbacks?

"He was a fiery little dude," Matthews said. "There's never been a better competitor. He wasn't on the end of many losing ballgames his entire career. Bill was a rounder. Billy and Jerry Mazzanti, the big old tackle from Lake Village, they were Mutt and Jeff. Bill's about 5'10" and Jerry about 6'4". You'd go to Maxine's Taproom and you could have seen them about any time."

They also hung out in the old Rockwood Club, Matthews and MacKenzie learned to their chagrin.

"I remember MacKenzie and I one time thought we should check that place out," Matthews said. "We saw Moore and a bunch of them out there. Mackenzie said, 'Moore, we can't have this. You are supposed to be a damned leader. What kind of leader is this?' Billy says, 'I *am* a leader.'

"And MacKenzie said, 'Yeah, you are, but you're not the right kind. Hell, Castro is a leader, too. We don't need any of that kind.'"

Wilson laughed.

"But any of the players will tell you that Billy Moore was a leader," Matthews said. "Billy Gray must have told me a thousand times, 'Any time I stepped in the huddle, any damn thing Billy Moore said was going to happen, I believed it.'

"He was a competitor. I used to try my best in the off season to make him quit when I knew he had been partying. I poured it on. I made him carry two buckets of concrete on his back on a rod and carry it around the old basketball arena. But he never quit. You couldn't make him quit."

Billy Moore did take issue with Wilson's account of the Rockwood incident when it was brought up after Matthews's death.

"They didn't compare to me to Castro," Moore rebutted. "It was Al Capone."

Even Moore couldn't have been any more indefatigable than a player whose name eluded Matthews.

"I can't remember who the player was," Matthews said. "When practice was over I told him, 'You don't go to the damn dressing room. You start circling that practice field.' I told him, 'I may be back in 30 minutes, I may be back in an hour, or I may not be back until practice tomorrow. But when I come back, your ass had better be out here running.' I went on and I forgot about him. And then about eight o'clock it hit me. 'Damn! Reckon he's still out there?' I went out there, and he was still out there, blowing and going."

NEVER HOLD A GRUDGE

Regardless of who it was, no doubt Matthews gave him a pat on the back and a clean slate.

That's one thing that Matthews's players always assert: "Whenever Coach chewed you out in practice, and he may have chewed you out a lot, he'd always come back and talk to you before you left practice for the dorm."

Not holding grudges was as basic to coaching football as blocking and tackling, in Matthews's view.

"I learned that a long time ago," Matthews said. "I guess because I used to get my ass chewed out. And it came from Coach John Tucker [of Arkansas Tech] whom I thought more of than anybody outside of my dad.

"When I got my first coaching job, I asked Coach Tucker if I could visit with him. One of the things that stuck was, 'Don't get so involved with what you know and what you think you know that you think you are relating when you are not.' In other words, keep it simple. Another thing was, 'You can be just as tough on a kid as you want to be if they know it's not anything personal—that you are just coaching your way and you are trying to make them better. And if it gets too bad with a player, don't let the sun go down until you've gone to see him and visit with him.'

"I overdid it getting tough, I guess, sometimes. But I think the ones I rode the hardest probably think as much of me as the others, probably more. As long as you are fair and honest with them and tell it like it is...it may not suit them right then...but as they get older, they are smart enough to know it might help them. It helped me when I was coming up.

"The best thing about coaching is to have that kind of relationship and know that in some way you contributed to their overall success. I look at some who are pretty successful now and I know they gained confidence undertaking something...from football. They learned if you want something bad enough, hell, go after it. It may not be easy, but if it's easy, it may not be worthwhile."

That wisdom didn't go untapped.

Former players beat a path to his door for advice. So did coaches, including Houston Nutt.

"I told him at the beginning he had a number-one fan," Matthews said of Nutt in 1998. "But that I wasn't going to bother him. I won't be one of those kind of people. But if there's anything I can do or help you with, you know where I am. He'll come by a time or two. He knows where I stand."

Everybody knew where they stood with the coach who thought that telling it like it is wasn't a slogan, just the truth.

SWITZER GETS BAITED

B arry Switzer, who won three national champion ships as Oklahoma's head coach and a Super Bowl coaching the Dallas Cowboys, played for Wilson as a Razorback, coached with him as a Razorback assistant, and was conned by him.

"I got to know Wilson, both sides," Switzer said. "As a player, I played for him. He coached my position, linebacker. And I coached on the staff with him for six years. I knew how tough he was, yet at the same time I knew what it was like to be with him off the field and in the work room. He always had me go with him when he and [football assistant coach] Steed White and [basketball coach] Glen Rose would go on frog-gigging trips. He had me go because I was a young guy who could pick up the frog gigs, the boats, the batteries and lights while he, Glen and Steed White sat around and had drinks until it was dark enough to go gigging frogs.

"He was truly a unique old dinosaur. He won it his way. It might not fit today, but I would like to think he would have. There would have been enough to stick around who would respond to him. The rest would have left, but we still would have gone out and kicked somebody's ass."

In the meantime, Matthews touched his own teams' hearts after making them show more heart than they knew they had.

"A coach who has been around as long as he has," Switzer said, "touches a lot of people's lives. A college and high school coach's mission is to produce productive men for our society for 60 or more years of living for them and their families. The pro game is all about winning. But the college game is about developing young men, and that's what Wilson did. He touched a lot of men's lives and taught them how to be a man and how to live it. We'll miss him."

McDONNELL SEES BOTH SIDES

Two anecdotes by track coach John McDonnell tell volumes about Wilson going by what's right rather than what's expedient, whether it was leveling a big booster or sticking by a parking attendant doing his job.

"After I was promoted to head coach," McDonnell said, "a car was part of my salary. When we had Heather, we needed a four-door instead of a two-door. I called the dealer, who was from out of town. The guy really chewed me out and said, 'You don't like the car you got, then come down here and park it!' So I told Wilson about it."

Wilson was the man to tell, because he set the ticket seating priorities. Like most everything Wilson did, he dealt with it on the spot.

"Wilson wheeled around," McDonnell recalled, "dialed a number and said, 'I've got the track coach in here. What's this about the car?' For a while he's just saying, 'Yeah,' and 'Uh-huh,' while the dealer says his piece. And then Wilson says, 'Well, I tell you, either get him a four-door car or get your ass in the end zone!' And then he hung up."

John got the four-door but also got chewed out later.

"On Saturday mornings before football games," McDonnell said, "we weren't supposed to park in certain spots. I needed to park my truck for a couple of minutes to unload some Gatorade for the cross-country workout, but the kid on the gate didn't let me park and reported me. Wilson sees me that day at the game and roars, 'John what's this #@*? I tell those people not to let *anyone* park there. You could park your @#% truck up a block.' All I could say was, 'Coach, you're right,' because he was. I admire people like him who, if they have something to say, say it right to your face."

A lot of faces that Wilson Matthews burned with blue language mourn that they won't be burned again.

Mel McGaha

NOT EVERYONE PUTS THEIR PANTS ON THE SAME

Starring at Arkansas in football, basketball and baseball and later being a major-league manager for the Cleveland Indians and Kansas City Athletics, Mel McGaha learned well the old saying about "they all put their pants on the same way we do."

But in Mel's case, they didn't when he arrived at the UA in 1944.

"I came from Mablevale High School, and we didn't have a football team," McGaha said. "I came up for a basketball tryout for Coach Eugene Lambert. I worked out, and they gave me a scholarship. And I couldn't afford to go back home, because I didn't have enough money. I came up here with a $10 bill–that's all my dad could afford–and my clothes in a paper sack, and I hitchhiked up here. So I had to stay up here.

"The football players were coming in, and I found out they got $10 more a month than the basketball players did. And I said, 'Why can't I go out for football?' Boy, were they ever overjoyed. They needed someone to run at and run over. The only experience I had in football was from a tree looking over the fence at the games at Little Rock High School. Those were the only games I had seen."

He must have been bewildered on where to line up.

"Not only did I not know where to line up," McGaha said, "I didn't know how to put the uniform on. I didn't know what to get. They said, 'Everybody get in line and go

get your gear.' I had been listening to them talk. I found me
a guy who I had known had made All-State. So I figured if
anybody knew what to get, he would. So I got right behind
him. I stood in the middle of the floor and watched them
put stuff on so I would know where to put them on. It got
down to where I had just two pieces of equipment left, and
I didn't know where in the world they went. And by then,
everybody was out on the practice field. Of course I didn't
want everybody to know that I didn't know where to put
them on. So I just put them in the locker and went on out.
The second day we're having one-on-one tackling practice.
And this old boy from Arkansas City tackled me hard and
then slapped my thigh and said, 'Where are your thigh pads?'

"I said, 'So that's where they go. There ain't no place in
my britches for them.'

"He said, 'Yeah, there is. I'll show you when we get in.'
And he did, and he never told a soul. That was pretty good."

So was McGaha, though he modestly shrugs it off.

"My first game," McGaha aw-shucked, "I fooled a lot
of people that day."

Apparently Mel was good enough to fool a lot of the
people a lot of the time in a lot of things. He was voted into
the UA's Hall of Honor as a three-sport star.

McGaha died in the spring of 2002.

Bill Montgomery

Bill Montgomery

THE SHOOTOUT RELIVED–DAILY

During the Cotton Bowl week that Houston Nutt's 1999 Razorbacks capped by routing Texas, it seemed Arkansas lost daily to the Longhorns.

Every Cotton Bowl function had remembrances of Arkansas losing the 1969 Shootout, 15-14, to Texas.

Every day, especially at the big New Year's Eve Cotton Bowl luncheon that had a narrated film of every play, Dallas businessman and former Razorback quarterbacking great Bill Montgomery watched himself throw a critical interception when the Hogs were driving for what would have been the game-clinching score.

Razorback players, many not even born during the fabled Game of the Century that brought President Richard Nixon, Billy Graham and future president George Bush Sr., among others, to Fayetteville, resented the constant reminder of the Texas victory.

So did the late Wilson Matthews, then the Arkansas associate athletic director emeritus who walked out on the Cotton Bowl luncheon.

Montgomery, though, absorbed every bit of it without rancor.

"I didn't look at it as a torture week," Montgomery said. "It's a game the football world is not going to forget about.

"The reality is it was a heartbreak, more than that, the high point and the low point of my athletic career. The fact is it has stood the test of time as the game of the century. So if you played in the greatest one of all, that's something to be proud of. Of course I would have given up all that if we won the game. But we didn't. I don't think the Cotton Bowl meant it to be that Texas won the game. I think it was to congratulate both teams for participating in it. They want to say congratulations for playing in the greatest football game of all time, though I get as tired as everybody else watching the comeback."

The fact that Nutt's 1999 Hogs trounced Texas, 27-6, definitely cast a more favorable light on that whole week.

"Not only did we win," Montgomery said. "But we brought more fans to Dallas than the state university in Texas did. That's impressive."

DEFINED TOO MUCH BY '69?

Were Montgomery and those Razorbacks of Frank Broyles too heavily defined by that one '69 Shootout game?

"Those are questions there really isn't an answer to," Montgomery said. "Why do certain events capture the imagination? And in the world of college football, this game did capture the imagination of the nation. It continued to capture the imagination of fans and it will go on. So it may seem it gathers more importance than it deserves. And the fact is people like to talk about it and remember. And that's just a fact. For three quarters I played pretty well and I had a couple of mistakes at crunch time that were pretty costly for us. So I can stand in the blame line and I am certainly willing to do it. But regardless, my three years playing for Arkansas were fabulous in every respect. Being associated with the University of Arkansas and having the opportunity to play for the Razorbacks and Coach Broyles were highlights of my life that I will never forget. And taking the good with the bad, there was a lot more good than there was bad."

Those 10-1, 9-2 and 9-2 teams Montgomery quarterbacked from 1968-70 prove that.

"You think about it," Montgomery said. "We tied for the Southwest Conference our sophomore year. We lost to Texas in '69 and '70 and they won both national championships. We only lost five games and were in the top 10 every year. The list goes on and on with great things our teams accomplished. I'm very proud of the records we set and the record that we had. But having said all that, if I could go back and change one thing, I would have just as soon had one incomplete pass as not."

He meant that interception against Texas, of course.

The hype of the Shootout dwarfed what Montgomery thought was the biggest victory of his era, the 1968 Hogs beating Georgia, 16-2, in the Sugar Bowl.

"Georgia was undefeated when we played them in the Sugar Bowl," Montgomery said. "[Former Georgia coach and current athletic director] Vince Dooley said it was the greatest defensive team he ever had and I agree. They had a great defensive team. So to go to the Sugar Bowl and play an undefeated Georgia team and walk away with a victory, that was a great win for Arkansas and certainly ranks up there with a lot of great victories."

MONTGOMERY'S SHARE OF DICUS'S HONOR

When Montgomery's prime Razorback receiver, current Razorback Foundation President Chuck Dicus, was inducted into the College Football Hall of Fame, Chuck said he was kidded about Montgomery deserving a share of the trophy.

Montgomery said the honor was all Dicus's.

"Chuck would have got in the Hall of Fame with or without me," Montgomery said. "He was such a great player. Being able to have somebody like Chuck Dicus to throw to made all the difference in the world. He sort of made our passing game. The key to Chuck was he was fearless. He caught the ball over the middle with complete disregard for the bodies flying around. He had great quickness off the break. And he also had great hands. He didn't drop the ball. So you throw all those things together: great quickness, the ability to cut. He was not the fastest guy; his times were not that great. But he had good speed. Put a football in his hands and he got faster. You take all those things and roll them up into a package, you come up with a great football player. That's what Chuck was."

Dickey Morton

Dickey Morton

DICKEY MORTON REMEMBERS, SORTA

Dickey Morton remembers that eventual Minnesota Vikings all-Pro linebacker Matt Blair wasn't a linebacker when they met September 29, 1973, in Fayetteville.

That's about all Arkansas all-Southwest Conference running back Morton can remember about the meeting.

"He was a safety at that point," Morton said, "or a corner, one of the two. He kind of rattled my memory a little bit."

And rattled every fan in the place with as hard a hit as one can remember seeing and hearing at a football game.

"We were burning them on the option with the pitch on the sweep," Morton said. "He was going to take me out of the play regardless if I got the ball. Mike Kirkland was quarterbacking. I was looking at Mike, and Blair came straight for me. So I'm looking at the ball coming into my hands. It hits my hands and I turn my head and that's it. I don't see nothing. And I didn't feel nothing. And the ball was still sitting in my hands. I was so relaxed. But I didn't hurt at all. I was fine. Of course I went about 10 yards backwards. But I was fine. Like I wasn't hit at all, like someone had laid me down with the ball there." Running back coach Richard Williamson immediately assessed the situation's true importance.

"All Coach Williamson said," Morton mused, "was 'Way to hang on to the ball.' And it was like, 'I did hang on to it, didn't I?'"

Morton went out for a while but came back in to win it for Arkansas, though the Hogs did have 12 men on the field when they scored the winning touchdown.

"I may have been the 12th guy," Morton said.

Clouded though his head might have been, it was reserve slotback Kelvin O'Brien who became the 12th man in an unplanned "slotbone" that the officials didn't detect when the Hogs switched from the "I" to the "wishbone" on the goal line. "We had the wishbone and two wideouts, too," Morton said. "Earle Bruce was their coach and he was throwing a fit. But the officials never saw it, and we won 21-19. Good ballgame; we needed it."

NEVER WISHED UPON A BONE

"We had lost twice running the wishbone in 1973 when we didn't have the players to run it," Morton, a Dallas scatback who excelled as an I-formation tailback said. "I'm not a wishbone blocking back; that's why I didn't go to Texas. And we didn't have any fullbacks." Or much of anything else. After 17-0 and 38-6 losses to Southern Cal and Oklahoma State, the wishbone was out and a lot of freshmen were in.

"We had 17 freshmen start that year," Morton said. "That's a lot. But I was happy to have guys of that caliber no matter what they were. My deal then was, 'I don't care what you are, I want the best player out there. I don't care if it's a mature guy or a freshman; put the best guy out there.'"

Morton was their best guy, no question. Virtually on his own, the scatback set a Razorback record with 271 yards rushing in 1973 during a 13-7 victory over Baylor in Waco.

"I had an upset stomach," Morton recalled. "I had 200 yards at halftime, threw up on the sidelines, felt better and ran 71 more. I would have had more, but one play I ran wrong and had to eat it."

Baylor's quarterback set records that day, moving the ball up and down the field, but couldn't put it in the end zone.

During Morton's three years, 1971-73, the Razorbacks beat every SWC team at least once except for one–the lowly, hapless Rice Owls were 2-0-1 on the Hogs during that stretch.

"There was a breakdown somewhere," Morton said. "Because they shouldn't have been close to us."

Houston Nutt

Houston Nutt

HOUSTON PLAYS
FOR FRANK AND LOU

Long before he took Arkansas by storm as the Razorbacks' new head football coach in 1998, Houston Nutt captured the state's imagination as a heralded quarterback recruit out of Little Rock Central for Frank Broyles's Razorbacks in 1976.

In one game of '76, starting in place of the injured Ron Calcagni to quarterback a 46-14 Southwest Conference rout of TCU, Nutt lived up to that billing.

"That was an awesome feeling," Nutt recalled of that SMU game. "Coach Broyles said, 'Today's quarterback is going to be Houston Nutt. He's won a lot of games. And he's got great support around him and we're going to win.' And we did. After the first series of the third quarter I was out of the game. We beat them bad. I was signing autographs after the game. That was one of the highs of a very difficult year. It was Coach Broyles's last year."

The Hogs, losing Calcagni for the season later on, wallowed to 5-5-1 after a 5-1 start.

Athletic Director Broyles replaced himself as head coach with Lou Holtz in 1977.

"The next year was a rude awakening," Nutt recalled. "Coach Holtz coaching spring ball was just amazing. He put a lot of pressure on everybody. But he played me the third series every game. Some games I would play two, three, even six series. The biggest satisfaction was taking the second group down the field to score against Texas A&M. That was a big win on the road."

Nutt quarterbacked the third series, plus much of the second half, in the 31-6 upset of mighty Oklahoma at the Orange Bowl.

"We get down there in Miami," Nutt recalled. "And we're scrimmaging every day and they show pictures of OU in shorts on the beach. And we had lost [All-American guard] Leotis Harris to a knee injury in the last scrimmage in Fayetteville, and then Coach Holtz suspended [leading running backs Ben Cowins and Micheal Forrest and receiver Donny Bobo]. It was the biggest game of our lives, and we had to wait for the kickoff because of an overlapping game on TV. I remember Coach Holtz saying, 'Does anybody have some jokes?' We've got time to kill for about seven minutes. Finally [punter] Bruce Lahay said a terrible joke. And we all started laughing because it was such a bad joke. We were loose and confident that night."

That Orange Bowl marked Nutt's last Razorback game.

He transferred to Oklahoma State, knowing that the next year at Arkansas he would be No. 3, not only behind Calcagni, but behind Kevin Scanlon, Holtz's quarterback at North Carolina State who redshirted in '77 upon transferring to Arkansas.

"As a redshirt," Nutt recalled of Scanlon, "[Holtz] let him have practice time. He couldn't play that Saturday, but he'd get practice time. It would be, 'Calcagni, out! Houston Nutt, out! Give me Scanlon!' So that's going to build up morale. But he was sending a message to me and Cal."

Ironically, Scanlon, a sports agent for Stephens Sports Management, became Nutt's agent when Houston became Arkansas' head coach.

Nutt's reasons for leaving the UA ran deeper than being third to Calcagni and Scanlon.

"We had a difficult relationship," Nutt confessed of himself and Holtz. "Because when we got off the bus in

Little Rock, it was always, 'Hey, are you going to play Nutt?' There was an instant strain. And he was playing the right guy in Ron Calcagni. No doubt. And he played me in every game. But there was a constant strain."

Of course it was a strain to be an assistant coach for Lou, much less play for him.

Coaches could get banished to the sidelines just like players during one of Lou's tirades.

"I've never seen a guy that would run off a Larry Beightol, a Don Breaux and a Ken Turner," Nutt recalled. "Tell them to go to the stands. The best coaches I'd been around in my life, and he'd tell them, 'You had your chance. I told you yesterday we're not getting it done, and here we are today not getting it done. I'll get it done! You go to the stands and watch me coach. I'll coach them all.' I thought that was pretty harsh for coaches we all respected, to send them into the stands.

"One thing I appreciate was [offensive line coach] Larry Beightol in 1977. We were beating TCU like 35-0 or something. During the week we were told, 'If they get in an eight-man front, check down the line and throw the post. I come down the line, fake the veer and throw the post-touchdown. And [Holtz] is waiting on me as I'm coming off the field.

"'What are you doing?'

"'All week long you told me to check.'

"'I told you the last two or three series do not check to a pass. We're up 35 points!'

"And Larry Beightol got in there and said, 'Look, you always are getting mad at him that he's doing it wrong. The guy made a touchdown!'

"So you remember things like that, an offensive line coach like Larry Beightol taking up for me. I really appreciated that. Ken Turner was the same way."

LEARNING LOU'S LESSONS

Though their relationship was strained during Nutt's season of being Lou Holtz's Razorback backup quarterback, their mutual respect never wavered.

In 1983, Holtz summoned the quarterback who had left him to be a Razorback graduate assistant coach, an assignment for which Nutt said he's been eternally grateful.

And although he's marketed as 'Nuttin' But Fun,' Houston showed he's learned to be Lou when it suits him, as in readying the 1999 Hogs for their 27-6 Cotton Bowl trashing of Texas after their sorry regular season ending performance in a 35-10 loss to a 3-8 LSU team in Baton Rouge, Louisiana.

"That LSU game before we went to the stadium," Nutt said, "I saw more grandmothers and relatives in the lobby. We were more worried about where we were going to go after the game, because they were 2-8. And they were waiting for us to beat them, but then it was like, 'If you all don't want to take it, we will.' And they did.

"So right after that we went the Lou Holtz route. We went hard for 20 days. No off days–weight room, practice–always something. A couple of seniors said, 'Coach, can we take a couple of days?' I said, 'No, you don't deserve it. I got a bad feeling in my stomach and we are going to do something right.'"

A COTTON BOWL BANQUET SETS UP A FEAST

"I could tell we were more focused when we got down to Dallas," Nutt said of what led up to the Hogs' 27-6 Cotton Bowl clobbering of Texas. "But what probably helped the most was the banquet the day before the game."

Arkansas' associate athletic director emeritus, Wilson Matthews, called the luncheon a "damn Texas pep rally" as the Hogs and their official party were subjected to a near ceaselessly running film of Arkansas' heartbreaking 1969 loss to Texas, sandwiched between malaprops at Arkansas' expense.

"First they don't say we're from Arkansas," Nutt recalled of the luncheon's emcee. "They say we're from Arizona. Texas's highlights were much bigger than ours when they showed the teams' highlight films. And they showed that '69 game the whole time.

"I'll never forget that meeting the Friday night before the game. I said, 'We've had a good month, guys. We haven't won a bowl game in 15 years and they don't expect you to win one now.' And [senior receiver] Anthony Lucas says, 'Coach, I just want to say one thing. They didn't know your name today; they called you Dennis Nutt. They didn't know our name. They called us Arizona. All they did was show the '69 game, and then when they did show the team highlights, their highlights were much longer and better. But tomorrow when the game ends around 1:30 pm, they are going to know who we are.'

"They hit the room. There was no need for bed check that night."

EXPECTING THE WORST

Some of the best news that Houston Nutt received during the week of Arkansas' January 1, 2000 Cotton Bowl victory over Texas had nothing to do with the game.

Nutt received a knock on his Hyatt hotel room door in Dallas from a hotel manager.

Hotel managers knocking on coaches' doors seldom come bearing glad tidings.

"I mean when he knocked on my door," Nutt said in the summer of 2000, "I thought it was, 'Okay, somebody must have thrown somebody off the balcony.' But he's telling me how well behaved they are. That was the greatest compliment when the hotel manager at the Hyatt said, 'I've been doing this with the Cotton Bowl for 10 years. Without a doubt this is the most well mannered, best behaved team that has stayed here.' That means a lot, almost as much as beating Texas. Danny Ford left me some good players, no doubt about it. The last two years they have been bona fide football players with character."

NUTT RETURNS TO HARD TIMES

After his year as Lou Holtz's graduate assistant in what was to be Holtz's final Razorback campaign, Nutt left Ken Hatfield's first staff as a graduate assistant in the spring of '84 to become a full-time assistant at Oklahoma State.

He didn't return to Arkansas again until 1990 as the receivers' coach for Jack Crowe, the offensive coordinator promoted to head coach when Hatfield left in late January for Clemson.

Houston was shocked to see what Crowe inherited, even before those 1990 Hogs went 3-8.

"You start as a graduate assistant at Oklahoma State under Jimmy Johnson," Nutt recalled, "[and] come back as a grad assistant under Lou Holtz in his worst year. And then you come back in '90 and it's hard times, tough times, people mad. For me finally to come back to Arkansas as an assistant after being at Oklahoma State for seven years, so pumped up, but then to see what we had. That was the biggest shock of my life. I can't believe this. We had better at Oklahoma State!

"But there's not a price you can put on that for handling difficult situations. Like in 1999 after the Ole Miss game. We lose 38-16 in Oxford. It was 'Hey, you've got a great opportunity. We're getting to play Tennessee this week. Nobody thinks we're going to do it, but we're going to do it.' And we did [28-24]. But if we didn't have those experiences, I would have panicked."

Crowe's Hogs went 3-8 and 6-6 in 1990 and '91, and then it was hit the road, Jack, one game into 1992. Broyles sent Crowe flying following the 10-6 season opening shocking loss to The Citadel at Fayetteville. Defensive coordinator Joe Kines became the interim coach for that 3-7-1 season and was replaced by Danny Ford two days after the season ended.

Nutt left shortly thereafter to become the head coach at Murray State. He left still harboring Citadel memories, especially when his 1998 Hogs debuted against underdog Louisiana-Lafayette.

"We're riding the bus from Bentonville to Fayetteville," Nutt recalled of head coaching his first Razorback game. "And I'm not believing this is getting ready to happen. We're going to run through this 'A'. We start thinking, 'Have we prepared well enough?' And thoughts of The Citadel come to mind. And all these emotions that you've thought about the Hogs since you were six years old, you know it's coming. You want to give a good show and let them be proud. But after the kickoff and then we score first, all that nervousness goes out and it's just let the players play. They are ready."

LEAVE THE LIGHT ON FOR HIM

Tom Bodet can bet on a sure thing if the Razorbacks ever play in another Las Vegas Bowl.

"If we ever go there again," Nutt said, "we'll probably stay out of town. We'd go out in the desert somewhere and find us a Motel 6."

No Caesar's, Maggio's or Golden Nuggets. The bright lights of Vegas and the freedom he gave the Hogs to enjoy them sapped his team in the 31-14 Las Vegas Bowl loss to UNLV in December of 2000.

"I would handle it so much different," Nutt said. "To play the UNLV guys there, what a trap. The bright lights where nothing closes; UNLV's guys are used to it. We weren't mentally ready. And the crowd is nothing, and all week they've been saying, Mountain West, SEC. No comparison. I told the staff Wednesday or Thursday, 'I don't feel good.' We were practicing good, but the atmosphere, there was just that feeling that all we've got to do is show up. But at halftime we knew we were in trouble when they tied it up."

LOWEST OF THE LOWS

As excruciating as losing 28-24 to Tennessee on a fluke fumble in 1988, and as angry and embarrassed as he was that his 1999 Hogs lost by routs at Ole Miss and at Baton Rouge to a bad LSU team that had just fired its coach, Nutt said the Las Vegas Bowl loss was the "most disappointing."

"You just felt so bad that whole off season," Nutt said. "You saw some attitude problems we had to correct."

TWO BEST YEARS

O f his four seasons, Nutt looks back most fondly on 1998 and 2001.

"The first year, I had such unbelievable kids who were so hungry," Nutt said. "The previous staff had the recruiting, the toughness and character all there. They just needed that much confidence to get over the top. It was perfect for a new coach. Those kids had been through the wars–Brandon Burlsworth, Russ Brown, Chad Abernathy, Grant Garrett, Chrys Chukwuma, David Barrett, Kenoy Kennedy..."

SMU, an upset victor over Hogs from 1995-97, the last two years convincingly, was the crossroads game, two games into '98.

"SMU," Nutt said, "we told them it wasn't going to be close. We jump 10-0 and they tie it 10-10, and it could have gone either way. Our sideline, I think I told Joe [Ferguson, the quarterbacks coach] on the phone in the press box, 'These guys think we're going to lose the game. You ought to see their eyes.' But once we got over [winning 44-17] and beat Alabama out here. That was the most solid game; we had offense, defense and kicking game where we actually made a team quit, 42-6, right here. It was our team right there. The cord was cut with the previous staff, and they trusted us and we trusted them. There was a bond."

A bond that still holds even with the team's greatest player, All-American Burlsworth, killed in an automobile accident.

"Russ Brown, Abernathy, Grant Garrett and Burlsworth's mother," Nutt said in the summer of 2002, "I talk to them probably once a month to this day. That is a great, great feeling."

Those '98 Hogs finished 9-3 with a loss to Michigan in the Citrus Bowl.

The Citrus was a great bowl, but Nutt says the Hogs were just a couple of plays away from 11-0 and having a rematch with eventual national champion Tennessee in the SEC championship game.

"What makes you sick," Nutt said, "is we probably could have been in the real game, the way things were falling. We make three critical mistakes against Tennessee or it's going to be a blowout. We win that, and then I ought to kick myself for the Todd Latourette deal."

Placekicker Todd Latourette was charged with DWI but was acquitted.

The day after Latourette was charged, Nutt suspended him from the Mississippi State game, which Arkansas lost, 22-21, at Starvkille.

"The next week charges were dropped," Nutt said, "and we had six opportunities to kick a field goal."

THE COMEBACK OF 2001

Even after the Las Vegas Bowl loss, Nutt never heard criticism like he did early in 2001.

The Hogs needed a down-to-the-wire drive to eke by UNLV, 14-10, in the season opener at Little Rock and then lost three SEC games: 13-3 in Fayetteville to Tennessee, 31-10 in Tuscaloosa to Alabama, and 34-23 in Athens to Georgia.

They would finish 7-5 and stay within hailing distance in a 10-3 Cotton Bowl loss to Oklahoma, the 2000 national champion.

"You had 0-3 after barely winning that first one," Nutt said. "Then came 9/11. What could be worse for America? It was a terrible feeling."

The whole country had to rebound in their own way. The Hogs did with football.

"What you love about football is you persevere," Nutt said. "And after the Georgia game, I really thought we had a good chance. We should have beaten Georgia. We had them on the ropes and let them slip. But you could see the improvement. And then it started paying off.

"Coach Broyles did a remarkable thing, because we actually were supposed to play North Texas in December. After the game with [Georgia], the game was canceled because of 9/11. Right in deer season, you know nobody is going to come up Dec. 10 or whatever when that one was going to be rescheduled. So he instead got us to play Weber State on October 6.

"We needed a game like Weber State [a 42-6 victory in Fayetteville] when we played them. We needed a confidence builder in the worst way. We got it. We won, but we didn't look that good on film, so we could still get on them.

"And then we had two weeks to prepare for Lou Holtz. We won, and we got on a roll, got some unbelievable confidence and beat Auburn. Go to Ole Miss and we're not a good road team, but we win a road game and we're sky high. The only reason we beat Mississippi State [24-21 in Fayetteville] is because of confidence. Mississippi State is supposed to win that game. They score with 1:12 left and we score in 47 seconds. That's confidence. Matt made that long draw and changes the end of the field and is tired. We put Zak Clark in and he hits a 10-yard pass. Put Matt back in and it's a touchdown with Cedric Cobbs on a shotgun read."

Two things had much to do with salvaging the season.

Clark, now at UCA but the Razorback starter last season, and Jones blended into a two-headed quarterback, and a lot of freshmen whom Nutt, at one time, wanted to redshirt took a hand in actively changing the Hogs' 2001 fortune.

"That two-quarterback thing developed on its own," Nutt said. "The one plan we did have coming into the Georgia game is redshirting is out. Keep our team together and play the best players–Matt Jones, Shawn Andrews, all those guys...Although Shawn was actually before that. Birmingham, Pierce, Batman...forget about the redshirt. The time is now."

Leroy Pearce

VEHICULAR MADNESS

The late Bowden Wyatt, some unforgiving veteran Razorback fans remember ruefully, drove the car they had given him to Tennessee, never to return.

Leroy Pearce, now a longtime Fayetteville landlord, was an assistant to Wyatt, the University of Arkansas head football coach in 1953 and '54 after the 2-8, 5-5 and 2-8 nadir of Otis Douglas.

Wyatt's '54 Hogs, picked last in the Southwest Conference by prognosticators, went 8-3, won the SWC, and played Georgia Tech in the Cotton Bowl on January 1, 1955. Boosters were so grateful to Wyatt and his fabled "25 Little Pigs" that they gave him a Cadillac. Wyatt motored the Cadillac to Knoxville. Tennessee called the former Vol home to be their head coach.

Pearce, a former player and assistant under Wyatt at Wyoming, went with him to UT.

"He really didn't want them to give him a Cadillac," Pearce said. "They insisted on doing it for him. When he accepted it, it wasn't a [sure] thing he was going to Tennessee. We didn't know it at the time. But he told them, 'This is for what we have done, not what I'm going to do.' In other words, 'We won games this year, we might not win them next year.' But when we went to Tennessee, everybody translated that to 'He already knew he was going to go and took the Cadillac.' That was a very controversial thing."

For an Arkansas program desperate to win, Wyatt's two years were worth losing a fleet of Cadillacs.

"He was a good football coach," Pearce said. "A disciplinarian, and I think the greatest leader of men I've ever seen. I think every football player that played for him will speak very highly of him."

EVERY ISN'T NECESSARILY MANY

There just weren't that many players to tell about Wyatt during his Arkansas tenure. The 1954 team's 25 Little Pigs were the 25 Little Pigs because so many Piggies went home.

No vegetarian ever abhorred beef like Bowden Wyatt. Too much beef on the football body, that is.

Wyatt's grueling spring practice to extract the beef that Douglas doted upon trimmed the roster even more than it trimmed pounds. Many forsook football, fleeing into the night.

"I lived in the dormitory with the football players," Pearce recalled. "They were all required to eat breakfast. Usually they would leave in the middle of the night, and you wouldn't know they were gone until they missed breakfast. You'd check their rooms after breakfast and they would have packed and gone. The first thing asked me when I went to the office was, 'Well, who did we lose last night?' It was tough."

Eddie Bradford, one Wyatt inherited from Otis Douglas, recalled nightly being near tears from Bowden's Boot Camp. Richard Simmons's feel-good exercise it was not.

"Eddie was 235 or 240 for Otis Douglas," Pearce recalled. "He played here for us at 185. We had to get a lot of them down. Otis Douglas was a pro coach, so he had them all as big as houses. Our players were really in shape. We went for quickness instead of bigness."

The difference showed in the record, though not immediately.

"Arkansas had not won a game in the state of Texas for five years," Pearce said. "And we didn't win there our first year, either. So that was six years of no-matter-who-you-played-in-Texas, you lost."

SORRY, PREZ

Everyone but Wyatt went ga-ga over the first Hog win at Austin since 1937.

Bradford remembered that after the game, the Hogs took a train from Austin to Muskogee, Oklahoma, because Wyatt hated to fly. The mayor of Prairie Grove tried to stop the bus to read a proclamation to the team.

"'Don't stop the damned bus,' Wyatt roared," said Bradford. "'Run over him if you have to. But don't stop the bus.' We went straight to the fieldhouse and worked out."

Pearce didn't remember that, but he did recall, "The president of the University, Dr. Caldwell, met us at Muskogee and wanted Coach Wyatt to ride back with him. Coach Wyatt said, 'This is my team. I'll ride back with my team.'"

Allen Petray

Allen Petray

LA-LA in LA-LA LAND

A llen Petray could imitate Frank Broyles better than the Arkansas coach could be himself.

In fact, the young sophomore offensive lineman probably would have found it easier to imitate Broyles on national television than to start in the Razorbacks' first two games in 1973, when they were so overmatched against Southern California out at the Los Angeles Coliseum and against Oklahoma State in Little Rock.

"The '73 USC game in the Coliseum was surreal," Petray said. He was just over a year out of Malvern High School when he played against USC. "We were goggle-eyed being out in La-La Land and all that implies. We worked out in the Coliseum on Friday and freaked out at just being there, plus [we were] scared out of our minds at the likelihood of getting beat 62-6 or something like that."

It was a young line that would get younger two games later.

"Mike Parmer, Ron Fulcher and Randy Drake," Petray said. "All of us were making our first starts on the line. Game night we warmed up at the open end of the stadium, but there was temporary seating beyond the end zone–close, and major hecklers. One kept yelling at Fulcher, 'Hey, 69! You even look like a pig!' In the tunnel toward the dressing room Fulcher asked, 'Did you hear that?' Randy Drake said, 'Nothing you haven't been told by us already.'

"A Lynn Swann 80-yard punt return was negated because I was clipped–my crowning contribution to the game."

Arkansas lost, 17-0.

WORSE TO COME

The 17-0 loss to one of the preseason national championship picks seemed like a victory compared to the unexpected 38-6 shellacking Oklahoma State put on the Hogs the following week in Little Rock.

"[USC] had defensive speed best compared with the Miami U defenses in the late '80s," Petray said. "Super fast linebackers, ends and cornerbacks–flew to the ball. They didn't stunt on the line much, run or pass, because they didn't have to. Consequently the O-line graded well because we were blocking a fairly simple scheme. We sustained enough drives to use the clock, missed some close scoring opportunities, etc."

He paused.

"Oklahoma State saw this all on film. They threw every conceivable stunt at us: linebacker and secondary blitzes, cross stunts, standing nose guard, eight-man lines, etc., ad nauseum. We couldn't pick it all up; neither could the coaches, and so the story goes of moving an all-freshman line in [and] moving the rest of us out, relegated to special teams duty. After a week of private discussions regarding transferring to other schools, running a turkey farm, etc., we all stayed, curiously, all the way through our senior years. To this day, I don't know why."

Loyd Phillips

Loyd Phillips

HEALING THE
OUTLAND TROPHY WINNER

F reshmen weren't even allowed in the training room, Arkansas associate athletic director Bill Gray recalled of the days when the late Bill "Groundhog" Ferrell was the trainer.

But Gray, a Razorback quarterback-safety from 1961-64, said some veterans like Outland Trophy defensive lineman Loyd Phillips were training room regulars.

"Every day," Gray recalled, "Loyd would come in the training room complaining about something–his head hurt, his ankle was bad, something. And every day Groundhog would give him some pills and Loyd would say how much better he felt.

"So one day I asked Groundhog, 'Can I try some of those?'

"I did. They were just sugar pills."

Cliff Powell

FRANK'S CENTENNIAL

C liff Powell, former Razorback linebacker and Hall of Honor member, waxed clever when he brought down the house addressing the Razorbacks' centennial football celebration banquet in 1994.

"Chuck Dicus, Bill Montgomery and I had the opportunity to be involved in three historic events," Powell told the centennial banquet. "One, we played in the 100th year of college football, 1969. We all made Arkansas' All-Century team. And we'll still be around for Frank Broyles's resignation, which is tentatively scheduled for his 100th birthday."

Jon Richardson

Jon Richardson

ROLE MODEL

With black Razorback football stars abounding from the mid 1970s on, it's easy to forget there wasn't always a Jermaine Petty, a Wayne Martin, a Leotis Harris, a Henry Ford, or a Jimmy Walker being named All-American from the UA or eventual NFL stars like Steve Atwater, Kenoy Kennedy, Jerry Eckwood, Dennis Winston and Gary Anderson brightening the seasons.

But there wasn't a black scholarship football player in sight at the UA until 1969. That's when Frank Broyles and his staff recruited running back Jon Richardson out of Little Rock's Horace Mann High School.

Richardson didn't have the UA career of the aforementioned Razorbacks, but he had a good one both on and off the field. Because he was the first, he had an impact greater than all of them, especially in Arkansas' black communities.

Marcus Elliott remembers. Currently a Little Rock businessman and popular radio sports talk show host, the former Razorback All-Southwest Conference offensive guard first lettered at the UA some 10 years after Richardson played his last Razorback game. Yet to Marcus, Jon Richardson was and always will be a "larger than life" figure.

"I was five years old," Elliott recalled. "Jon Richardson spoke and was signing autographs at the Mount Pleasant Baptist Church. I brought a notepad, and he signed it. I brought my Bible, and he signed it. I even asked him to sign my hand. They used to tease me that I didn't wash my hands for two weeks. He was my first hero. To everyone in the black community he was a superstar. Number 24."

Clyde Scott

Clyde Scott

MISS ARKANSAS RECRUITS FOR THE HOME TEAM

Miss Arkansas did more than represent Arkansas beautifully in 1946.

She recruited perhaps the greatest athlete in Razorback history.

Clyde "Smackover" Scott, the Smackover, Arkansas product who would be an All-American running back, an NCAA champion, and a U.S. Olympic silver medalist hurdler, shipped out of the Naval Academy in Annapolis, Maryland to the UA because he met Miss Arkansas.

"The true story is I met my future wife there," Scott said of the former Leslie Hampton. "They had Miss Arkansas visit the Naval Academy, and I was her escort. The war was over, and we decided we wanted to be married, and you couldn't be married and stay in the Naval Academy. So that's why I finished my career at Arkansas."

TAKE ME OUT TO THE BALLGAME

Clyde Scott didn't get to do what he wanted to at Arkansas under football coach John Barnhill, despite being the envy of the Razorback athletes of his time.

"I really wanted to play baseball," Scott said. "Smackover had a men's team that I had played on. I wanted to play baseball real bad, but Barnie said, 'Nope. You can run track, but you are here to play football.'"

COACH SCOTT

As a Razorback hurdler, Scott was self-taught. "We didn't have a track coach when I was there. Hobe Hoosier was a line coach Barnie brought in from Tennessee. He was not a track coach, but he was who we had because they didn't have a budget for a track coach. We didn't even have a track in high school, but I started hurdling back then. The only true tracks I ran on were Camden for the district meet and the state meet."

What a spectacular track career Scott had as an Olympic silver medalist, launched from no track and no track coach.

"I guess it was at that," Scott said modestly.

Gerald Skinner

Gerald Skinner

SHAKING OFF THE SIGNS

We're used to watching pitchers shake off a catcher's sign in baseball, but how often in football does an offensive tackle shake off a sign from an offensive guard?

Quite often in one game, Arkansas offensive tackle Gerald Skinner recalled shaking off the X-block signal of Razorback offensive guard Greg Koch.

X-block meant the tackle blocked a linebacker instead of a defensive tackle.

Koch wanted Skinner to X, so Skinner, not Koch, would have to contend with Southern California linebacker Richard Wood during part of the Razorbacks' stunning 22-7 season opening victory over the eventual 1974 national champion Trojans.

"In front of me was Gary Jeter, who was an All-American tackle," Skinner said, "and in front of Greg was Richard Wood, an All-American linebacker. Those guys were so good. But Greg, you know him, he was just talking that stuff to them and making them so much madder. I finally told him, 'Be quiet so we at least have a chance of blocking them.' But we did have an X block. Greg would call X, and I would have to say yes or no.

"The first time I went up on Richard Wood, he creamed me. Greg called it again, and Richard Wood just smacked me. The third time I said, 'No.' I didn't want to block him anymore. And Greg said, 'Yes.' And I said, 'No.' Southern Cal had to be thinking, 'What the hell?'

"I remember we scored and Greg coming up the field in Richard Wood's face, talking to him awful. And Richard Wood just looked at him and said, 'It's a four-quarter ballgame.' And the next play Anthony Davis ran it back 98 yards. And I thought it really would be one of those days. But we won, and it became a win we'll remember forever and ever."

Barry Switzer

SWITZER COULD HAVE AVOIDED ORANGE BOWL AMBUSH

Crossett's Barry Switzer, the captain of Frank Broyles's 1959 Razorback Southwest Conference champions, three-time national championship coach with Oklahoma and Super Bowl championship coach with Dallas, almost came home to coach the Arkansas team to which his Sooners eventually lost, 31-6, in the January 2, 1978 Orange Bowl.

Broyles talked to Switzer before replacing himself with Lou Holtz as Arkansas' head coach.

"Frank offered me the job when Lou came," Switzer said. "Frank and I talked about it [for] about three days. I thought about it. Kay [Switzer] was from here, but remember we had just won two national championships and I had just recruited a great class–Billy Sims, Thomas Lott, Kenny King, Greg Roberts, the Tabor Twins, Darryl Hunt, George Cumby. The *Dallas Times-Herald* blue chip list had 19 players, and we signed 13 of them. So it would have been too tough to leave that bunch. We won three and probably should have won five or six. In '78 we should have beat Nebraska, but Billy fumbled at the one and we got beat, 17-14."

There was no doubt who won that '78 Orange Bowl, though the Sooners that Switzer coached, with Fordyce's Larry Lacewell as the defensive coordinator, were off-the-board favorites to whip the Hogs.

OU would have been heavy favorites even if Holtz hadn't suspended leading rusher Ben Cowins, fullback

Michael Forrest and leading receiver Donny Bobo for disciplinary reasons and if Arkansas All-American offensive guard Leotis Harris hadn't torn the anterior cruciate ligament in his knee during bowl practice.

Thomas Brothers

CAUGHT IN A TRAP

Playing tackle for John Barnhill's 1946 Razorbacks, Floyd Thomas recalled feeling trapped.

Especially when Barnhill trapped him with a wry quip after SMU kept running tackle traps.

"SMU ran a trap on us five times in a row," Thomas said. "And Barnhill told me, 'They got any cheese in that trap?' He took me out and put Chuck Liveley in. They got two guys, 250-pounders, running shoulder to shoulder at you. They can do anything they want to. They had a good football team."

Thomas, a McGehee native, recalled bending the rules to escape the trap sprung by Coach Matty Bell's Mustangs.

"One time in that trap they fumbled," Thomas said. "And I was trying to get the ball in the pileup, and I bent [this guy's] finger back. I had my hand on the ball and he had his body on it. He got a hand on it, and I got a hold of one his fingers and bent it back and got it before the referee, Ab Curtis, got to it. Ab always said, 'Watch your hands and feet,' when there was a pile. I gave it a pretty hard twist. I got the ball anyway. The guy griped, and the official said, 'I hear one word out of you and you'll sit next to Matty Bell. I figured that was a payback.'"

MUSCLED BY MUSCLES

Thomas, a center linebacker, said he seemed to absorb his hardest jolts against SMU, though perhaps the hardest came from his own teammate, Muscles Campbell.

"I intercepted a pass, and Muscles ran into me," Thomas said. "He got knocked out. The side of his helmet hit me on the shoulder pad. I hung on to the ball, but I sure didn't know what happened. I felt like the press box fell on me."

THE THOMAS BROTHERS

Billy Ray Thomas, Floyd's younger brother, transferred to Arkansas from Alabama and ended up being the starter in an alternating brotherly center linebacker tandem with Floyd in 1947. Billy Ray had the experience edge, since he only missed the 1945 season because of military service. Floyd missed 1943-45 as a World War II infantryman and then was miscast at tackle upon his Razorback return in 1946.

WASHING THE POUNDS AWAY

Billy Ray not only was Floyd's younger brother, but literally the little brother.

"Floyd weighed about 205, and I was about six-foot, 175," Billy Ray recalled. "I always lied on the weight. I would boost it by 10 pounds. Coach Barnhill said, 'Get on those scales.' It weighed 175 after I wrote down 185. Coach Barnhill said, 'What happened?' I said, 'Coach, I guess there was more dirt on me before I showered than I realized.' He just had that grin and said, 'Okay.' Those were good times."

TAKING LAND BY AIR

Billy Ray went air over Land in the 1946 Razorbacks' scoreless Cotton Bowl tie with LSU.

"In the Cotton Bowl they were on our goal line all day long and never scored," Billy Ray said. "They had one play where we had knocked the receiver out of bounds at the one. This tackle from LSU, Fred Land from North Little Rock, I knew they were going to try and smother me, because I was the smallest one on defense and they figured I'd just dive low and tie up a lineman so somebody else could make the play. So I faked low and jumped over him, and I hit the halfback on the four. That night at the banquet, Fred Land said, 'You were supposed to go under me and I was going to smother you.' I said, 'Oh, really.' He said, 'You son of a gun, I got my ass chewed out because I didn't block it!'"

Kendall Trainor

Kendall Trainor

IN A CLASS BY HIMSELF

Kendall Trainor stands in a Razorback class by himself.

Name another Razorback who has won a bowl game, played in the College World Series, and has a brother that is the UA's sports information director.

"I'm probably the [only] one in that category," Trainor said.

Kendall's field goal beat Arizona State, 18-17, for Ken Hatfield's Razorbacks in the 1985 Holiday Bowl. He played in the 1987 College World Series for Norm DeBriyn. And his younger brother, Kevin, became the UA's sports information director.

Kendall is no longer the answer to another trivia question: Who was the last Razorback whose points won a bowl game?

"I was tired of being the trivia question," Kendall said. "It's okay to be a trivia question for a couple of years, but after 15 years, that gets so old. I was so happy when they won the Cotton Bowl [over Texas on New Year's Day, 2000]."

BOWL VICTORY

Trainor was the happiest Hog when his 37-yard field goal with 21 seconds left beat Arizona State.

"That was the absolute highlight of my career," Trainor said. "One of the five biggest moments of my life outside my wife and kids. The last bowl practice we had, we ended on a field goal and I kicked [snapper] Richey Miller in the behind. That made it more pressure, because people on the sidelines were telling me not to think about it.

"Coach Hatfield was telling me a story about one of his Air Force kickers, trying to take my mind off it, and then realized the Air Force kicker had missed. He didn't finish the story. But what I thought about was a large-mouth bass. Bob Carver [a booster and the radio crew's spotter] asked me during practice what I was happiest doing, and I said, 'Bass fishing.' And he said, 'Just think of a large-mouth bass when you kick,' and I did."

The fish story made great postgame copy for the Holiday Bowl but started smelling like fish through his struggling Liberty Bowl performance to close 1987 and a struggling start as a senior in '88.

WIDE OF THE MARK

When he missed a short field goal just before half time in a September game against Ole Miss, Kendall started the second half by changing back to an old pair of kicking shoes. He dramatically threw the new pair he had used off the side of a trashcan on the sideline.

"My brother was in the stands," Kendall said, "and yelled, 'Even when you throw your shoes away it's wide right.'"

He had already caught halftime grief from kicking coach Ken Turner.

"He walked by my locker, called me a choker and kept walking," Kendall said. "I was steaming. But he's a great coach and a motivator from the old school like Coach DeBriyn. He knew what buttons to push. I told the team I would never miss another one. Some nodded, and others looked like, 'Yeah, whatever.'"

But he never missed again. Kendall kicked 24 straight field goals. He made All-American and scored the SWC champion Hogs' only points in a 17-3 Cotton Bowl loss to UCLA.

George Walker

A KNOCK-OUT

Rison's George Walker starred on Bowden Wyatt's fabled "25 Little Pigs," but before that, he had already made his mark with Larry Lacewell, the former Oklahoma defensive coordinator and Arkansas State head coach who emceed the banquet when Walker was inducted in the University of Arkansas Sports Hall of Honor.

"When I was a Fordyce Redbug, we played Rison," Lacewell said. "George Walker was their star, and we put money in a pot about who would knock him out of the game. I got the first crack, and I thought I splattered him. Except it knocked me 14 miles. One of the guys said, 'How was that?' I said, 'I'll tell you how that was. I want my money back. No one is going to knock him out of the game!'"

Walker humbly said the Hall of Honor was one game he didn't think he was fit to play.

"I was about to play golf the other day," Walker said, "and, as usual, at the very last minute I had to use the restroom. I raced down the hall, threw open the door and looked into the faces of three women. It did not take me long to realize I did not belong there. As I look down [at] these faces tonight, I have that same feeling. I do not belong here."

Dean Weber

FAINT PRAISE

Long and meritorious service can get you damned with faint praise by longtime Arkansas trainer Dean Weber.

Paying loving tribute to veteran Fayetteville orthopedist Dr. Tom Coker (called Old Tom by the UA staff to differentiate him from Young Tom, Coker's son, who is also an excellent orthopedist) Weber remarked, "He's nationally known for his expertise in treating feet and ankles. And he has the wisdom to know what he can treat and what should be referred to someone who may know something more in an area than he does. He has so much wisdom. Of course he should. He was the busboy at the Last Supper."

Now if Weber doesn't like you, there is no praise, faint or otherwise. Asked about the latest injury of an exasperatingly fragile former Razorback football player, Weber once replied, "She strained her wrist."

WHY IT WAS IMPORTANT

Fired the day after opening the 1992 season with a 10-3 loss in Fayetteville to The Citadel, a bewildered coach Jack Crowe said, "I didn't realize The Citadel game was important."

"It wasn't," Weber told him. "Until we lost it."

UNSOLICITED ADVICE

Ken Hatfield got all sorts of unsolicited advice during his Razorback coaching days, but a tip from trainer Dean Weber caught him totally off guard.

"Coach Hatfield never was one of the best dressed," Mark Calcagni, a quarterback of the Hatfield era, said. "He had this plaid jacket that might have been in in the late '70s. He wore it one time for a travel game. And Dean Weber asked him, 'Hey, Coach? Did you get dressed in the dark?' Coach Hatfield got a little upset. I think he thought it was pretty stylish."

Bob White

Bob White

SHEER LUCK

Long before he became a renowned Fayetteville attorney, Bob White was the subject of national publicity.

White lettered for Frank Broyles's Razorbacks as a placekicker from 1966-68. He kicked for some good teams, with the 1966 Hogs going 8-2 and the '68 Hogs going 10-1, tying for a Southwest Conference title and beating Georgia in the Sugar Bowl.

However, White got his publicity from kicking a bad field goal for a bad team.

It was the field goal that splashed the 1 on the 4-5-1 Hog record of 1967.

And it splashed, well, maybe inched is a better word, White into *Sports Illustrated*, courtesy of veteran Baylor coach John Bridgers.

"We're down 10-7 to Baylor and in a gully washer down there," White recalled. "We make a late last-minute drive in the rain and it's horrible. We get down to the goal line and can't get it in. Frank elects to kick a field goal from like the three. It's like a 21-yard kick. Glenn Hockersmith is one upback and Bruce Maxwell is the other one. For whatever reason, Hockersmith elects to line up on the wrong side of the ball. So we have no upback on the left side and two on the right."

Not a good omen on a clear day, much less so in torrential rain.

"We got no timeouts and the clock is running down," White said. "Terry Stewart is the holder, and we set the tee down and it's in the goo. On defense, they see there is no upback and they immediately shift into overload, and here they come. O'Malley snaps it and it's wet. I can't remember whether it hit the ground, but it doesn't get there. When Stewart puts the ball down on the tee, it slides off the tee and is laying there sideways.

"Here comes about five of them off their right side, which is our left side. They are laid out there to block it–nobody is there to stop them. I kick the ball, taking a divot like you would with a sand wedge.

"I kick the ball on its side, and somehow or other it goes underneath these guys who are laid out to block it–barely clears the linemen, and the reason it didn't get blocked at the line of scrimmage is everyone had moved over, and the ball gets up. It gets no higher than 11 or 12 feet at any time, and it nosedives and ducks over the left corner of the uprights.

"Tie 10-10. Bridgers has been around for years, and he's quoted later in *Sports Illustrated*: 'It was the worst looking field goal I've ever seen.'"

White said he couldn't disagree.

"It helicoptered over," White said. "A sheer stroke of luck."

Luck that was due that luckless team.

"We get out of there with the tie," White said. "And that was the infamous 4-5-1 year."

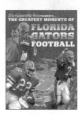
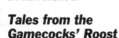